I0099128

Diary of a Silly Woman
Karen Roush

Why does a 50-something-year-old woman with four dogs and a beloved Volkswagen Beetle drive from Alaska to Mexico – and back?

Copyright C 2012 by Karen Roush

Published By OgDog Publishing House
ISBN-13 978-09969094108
ISBN-10: 0996094105

Printed in the United States

All rights reserved. No part of this book may be reproduced in any form or by any electronic or mechanical means, including information storage and retrieval systems, without permission in writing from the author.

Cover Design & Photos by Karen Roush

Main Characters:

A 50-something-year-old woman that prefers living on the edge

A 15-year-old parti-colored cocker spaniel called OgDog

An 11-year-old parti-colored cocker spaniel, Luce (OgDog's wife)

A 10-year-old parti-colored cocker spaniel, Woody Boy (their son)

An 8-something-year-old tri-colored basset hound called Zip Doodle, Zippy or DoDog—rescued into the world of wanderlusts

A 1998 white Volkswagen Beetle called VeVe

Table of Contents

Main Characters
Dedication
Introduction

Dedication

I became Silly Woman in my late 30's—well, maybe I always was one, but the title was passed on to me at that time. The original Silly Woman is my mother-in-law. It started when she would do something silly, like lock her keys in the car, fall off the dock while fishing with my 4-year-old son, trip on the 9th green right in front of the clubhouse, or spill her wine. You get the picture. When she would relay these incidents to the family, we would say in unison, "Silly woman!" Somewhere along the way, the title not only stuck, but it was expanded to include me as Silly Woman 2, and my sister-in-law as Silly Woman 3. Over the years we have had many laughs over Silly Woman, and that is how the title "Diary of a Silly Woman" came to be.

This book is dedicated to Irene Elizabeth Roush, my favorite and only mother-in-law, who taught me to age with grace, a sense of humor and a glass of Cabernet in hand.

Introduction

With a desire for a long road trip in early October 2008, my four dogs and I loaded up our beloved VW Beetle in Homer, Alaska, and headed south in search of the sun. I had leased my business, Tails-By-The-Bay Dog Camp, to a responsible couple for the winter, so we were free of responsibility and ready for an adventure.

Five days and 2,500 miles later, we were in Woodinville, Washington, visiting friends and looking for a winter place to live in the Seattle area. We stumbled onto the perfect house on Vashon Island, only a 20-minute ferry ride to West Seattle. There was also a cottage on the property leased to another free-spirited woman who would show me the island ropes and become my friend. The house was not available until November, so we continued our road trip across country to visit family in West Virginia for the next three weeks. Did I mention that trip was another 2,000 miles one way? In early November we made the trek back west to Vashon Island, ready to settle in for the winter.

My neighbor in the cottage next door and I quickly became friends based on an incident that happened early in our relationship. Little did I know this was just the precursor to an amazing adventure in Mexico.

Part I

Vashon Island, Washington

"Life is either a daring adventure or nothing"
—Helen Keller

Chapter 1 – The Wedding Gown Fiasco

Living on Vashon was close to Seattle and my art friends. One of my self-imposed projects was to collect recycled clothes and photograph myself in various attire. The idea was to eventually have a portfolio of images, and a recycled clothing store, online. One of my artist friends asked me if I would like her mother's 1949 wedding gown and her grandmother's crocheted dress (that she wore to the country club with Revlon Red lips and nails) to photograph and sell online.

I agreed during Thanksgiving dinner in Seattle, so she placed the clothing bag in the back of VeVe for me to take back to the island. A few days later I noticed it in the closet and carefully unzipped the garment bag. Grandma's dress was a medium-blue, fully crocheted A-line with short sleeves and a scalloped round neck that would look splendid with red lipstick and nail polish. There was no zipper, so I slipped it over my head and smoothed it down my body – it was the perfect fit.

I then pulled out the wedding gown and was amazed at just how beautiful it was. Fitted sleeves, with a side zipper and the most beautiful satin I have ever seen, with a long train, a teeny fitted waist and a beautiful full layered skirt—yards and yards of gorgeous lush material. I gathered the dress from the bottom and placed it on top of my head and began the process of pulling it down over my body. My arms were over my head to allow me to slip into the sleeves as I pulled the dress down. With the sleeves secured and the rest of the dress about halfway down my body, I suddenly realized there was no way in hell my chest was going to fit into the bodice. I would have to find a tiny model with a flatter chest to photograph in this dress.

Now, to get it off—try as I might, my arms were stuck straight up in the air and I could not wiggle them loose, nor could I lower them down. OMG! I could get claustrophobic if I don't figure something out soon. I can't force it because this is a vintage dress, probably worth at least $2,000, but more importantly, it belongs to my dear friend. If I pull too hard, it might rip at the seams. What the hell?

I am out in the country on Vashon Island, far from town and any friends, but I remember briefly meeting another lady living in the small cottage attached to my house. Maybe she can help? I carefully get down the stairs and out the door (opening it by bending at the waist and turning the knob with my outstretched hands), dragging the beautiful train behind. Thank God the lights are on in her cottage. I knock by tapping my foot against the door. I hear: "*Come in*," and only wish I could. I tap again and this time she opens the door to a crazed-looking blonde woman in a wedding gown half on with her arms reaching straight overhead, and beautiful satin material flowing everywhere—a strange site, indeed. She immediately starts laughing—at least she didn't slam the door in my face! "*Hey girl, I'm stuck! Can you help get me out of this dress?*" After oohing and aahing over the sheer beauty of it, she tells me we have to be careful not to rip the dress in the process. No shit! That's why I'm here, and my arms are killing me!

She grabs a chair to stand on so that she is higher than my head and tries to free my arms by inching the material along, finally concluding it's not really working. She evaluates the situation by walking around me, looks at all angles, and finally tells me to turn upside down, like touch my toes. Her theory is that we have to work with gravity to get the dress off. Okay fine, all modesty is already out the window. I hardly know this woman but I am on the verge of a panic attack that could cause me to rip this vintage gown off my body in a heartbeat if something doesn't give soon. I am close to tears, *"Please, just GET IT OFF ME!"*

I do as I'm told—turn over, touch my toes, and with her help, like magic, the dress slowly slides off my arms, over my head and into a heap onto the floor at my feet— unscathed. Thank God! I was free at last, albeit naked from the waist up. At least I was wearing a thong. She handed me a terrycloth robe. We looked at each other and collapsed into a fit of giggles, doubled over, holding our bellies as tears streamed down our faces. What a hell of a way to get to know your neighbor! But that night we were two women living next door to each other forever bonded by a 1949 vintage wedding gown.

Chapter 2 – Snow, Snow and More Snow! Seriously?

Fall is beautiful on the island, with lots of sunshine, until mid-December, when the snowstorm from hell hits the entire area. I thought I left winter in Alaska, but Vashon Island lost power and we are stranded off-island for over a week. Thank God for the Woodinville connection. I spent the holiday week with our dear friends, who graciously embrace me AND all my dogs. They are indeed kindred spirits and see the humor in just about everything. On Christmas Day, the storm raged on. The wind causes a large pine tree to blow over, landing on the porch and blocking the front door. We measured an unbelievable 2 feet of fresh snow on the deck as we helped guests climb through the snowdrifts and over the tree branches to get inside the warm and cozy house. We dined on the traditional turkey feast with local wine and decadent desserts. Life was good in Woodinville, no matter what the weather was doing outside!

In the next few days we were finally able to return to the house on the island. Over dinner with my landlady and neighbor I confessed that this was NOT what I had in mind for the winter, and we are going to have to go farther south—essentially giving notice after only two months. Her comment?

"Why don't you rent my casita in Guaymas?"

My response: *"You have one?"*

Enough said. A new plan was hatched over that dinner that ensured sun, sand and beach. The neighbor agreed to visit us in early February in time for carnival. After another glass of wine we envisioned a vacation of Girls Gone Wild in Mexico! It took no time flat to pack up VeVe and hit the road toward Tucson, where we would cross the border in search of paradise. We were given specific driving instructions to the rented casita that would become home for the next several months.

Perhaps you're wondering how to drive into Mexico with dogs? It's really rather simple: flash a big smile and say, *"Holá!"* Border patrol most likely will pet the dogs and wave you on through. I had my passport, health certificates for the dogs, and pesos in case I needed them. Nada. The officer asked where we were headed, smiled when I told him, and said, *"Have a good time, señorita."*

And, what about traveling as a single woman on the highway? No problem at all. I wouldn't do it after dark, but I left Tucson at 11 a.m. so had plenty of time to reach Guaymas before nightfall. With a full tank of gas, I had no reason to stop until I reached Casa Miramar in early evening.

Thus began the Mexican adventure that would be written about in a diary and posted daily on Facebook. Many people said they lived vicariously through these writings. Originally, they were called the Guaymas Chronicles, so imagine my surprise when I discovered that David Stuart had already written that book in the '70s.

Laughter is such good therapy and my stomach muscles were definitely toned after spending the winter at Casa Miramar. I simply laughed my ass off every day! I hope you enjoy reading about all the hilarious things that happened with Juanita, Maggie, four amazing canines, a white Beetle named VeVe and a Silly Woman. South of the border we found adventure in the land of sun, sand, tequila and beautiful people. It will remain a chapter in life that always makes me laugh out loud!

Part II

South of the Border

"I am thankful for laughter, except when
tequila comes out of my nose"
—Author unknown

Chapter 3 – Arriving in Guaymas

The five-hour drive from Tucson was scenic and warm. We made great time and arrived around 5 p.m. to a beautiful casita with bright colors and Mexican flair. It is so cozy and looks out onto a beautiful solar pool and a lovely patio perfect for outdoor living. The best part is the vibrant turquoise Sea of Cortez directly across the street. Zippy the basset hound is so excited with all the space and people—she can be at the pool, at the big house, in the casita or on the beach. She is totally exhausted tonight because she has been running from one place to the other, non-stop!

Janet, my landlady, greeted me with a wonderful chicken salad and a few margaritas. She told me about a local diet center, and weighing in every Monday. She has lost 10 pounds in two weeks. If I want to participate, I can go with her to meet the nutritionist and get started tomorrow. We agreed over our second margarita that getting in shape is a priority and hiring a personal trainer for daily boot camp is one way to get serious about it. She suggested Antonio, the caretaker of Casa Miramar and an integral part of her Mexican family. Antonio is here at least five days a week, and will keep us on top of our training regimen. If we can do it at home, we are more likely to be consistent and keep it up. And what a beautiful setting for exercise, around the pool. Oh, and by the way, Janet whispered, *"Please call me Juanita while we're in Mexico."*

I am told that a festival is being planned to welcome us to Guaymas—lots of people, food and drink. Guaymas is a charming Mexican community far removed from the tourist scene—just the kind of place to enjoy the sun, sand, and Mexican culture.

This is my schedule for the next few months:

1. Exercising and eating organic
2. Learning to speak some Spanish
3. Making pictures
4. Reading lots of books by the pool
5. Teaching yoga
6. Taking tennis lessons
7. Getting my bellybutton and ears pierced
8. Getting a tattoo

9. Getting my face waxed and my body massaged

10. Getting some metal taken out of my mouth

11. Drinking many margaritas to ease all the pain!

Life is as it should be in the moment here in Guaymas—sun, fun, beach and sand!

Chapter 4 - Beach Music

It is lovely here—warm during the day but sweatshirt weather at night. Dry heat, but never too hot, just right. With the sea across the street, the dogs and I were on the beach at 8 this morning. They love it; even OgDog, at almost 16, still enjoys the ocean. This is a neighborhood of rich Mexicans with only three American families in residence. A few doors down, the governor of Sonora has a second home, and the mayor lives here, along with other community business owners. It is a safe neighborhood and when the governor is here, there are bodyguards lining the streets—I'm sure you get the picture.

There was festive music playing until the early morning hours, and I fell asleep thinking how unusual this would be in an American neighborhood. Someone would probably call the cops!

But here, it is 'live and let live'—a zone of tolerance for one another.

This morning I learned a neighbor had hosted a "coming-out" party for their 15-year-old daughter. Earlier in the evening, Juanita and I had margaritas with dinner and then went to bed, or so I thought. Apparently, she got up a few hours later, put on her bathrobe and walked down the street to see where the beach music was coming from. The family pulled her inside, handed her a daiquiri and asked her to dance. She ended up having a truly fine time while I was asleep, only dreaming of dancing. Too funny, wish I could have been there. But there is always next time, and I am still getting oriented to the Mexican way of life.

Juanita is hosting a welcome-to-Guaymas party for me. It seems to be all about food, drink and party! Just like the Europeans. This is definitely my kind of place.

Chapter 5 – First Weigh-In

Let the diet and exercise program begin! Holy shit, we started running the beach this morning—well, I'm trying to run, if you can call it that. Most people walk faster than I run, but never mind. It gets my heart rate up, and that's a good thing, I think. So far it's run/walk for me but I will get there. I went to the diet center today with Juanita. Weigh-in was not pretty, OMG. Why do I weigh 10 more pounds than I did last year? The nutritionist activated two acupressure points for appetite suppression, laser-zapped me on the tummy to break up fat, and handed me a wallet-sized, preprinted card with week one diet plan—a choice of cereal with light milk or light toast with sugar-free marmalade, and fresh squeezed OJ for breakfast, and any meat (except pork) with green salad for lunch/dinner. Snacks include cucumbers and jicama dipped in salsa—that's it for the next week. Sounds simple. The good news is I can still have tequila, vodka, rum, gin and whiskey! Just no cervezas or vino.

There are so many dead pelicans and sea birds on the beach every morning. Apparently, the giant squids kill them. I was inspired to document them, so took my camera to the beach and photographed the surf washing over them. Their feet are an intense, beautiful blue like the ocean, and they look so peaceful in the surf. I am in awe of their beauty.

Chapter 6 - Dog Days in Mexico

Today, 15-year-old OgDog fell in the solar pool while I was inside (my worst fear). Juanita yelled that a dog was in the water and she thought it was Og. I flew out to the pool and pulled him out. He was swimming in circles but the paralyzed side of his head was in the water—ear down. I towel dried him and he immediately pooped; obviously it scared the shit out of him. After he calmed down, he was strutting around like his old self. Pretty worn out on this dog's day afternoon. He seems okay now.

This morning Woody was throwing up non-stop. I called a veterinarian, who spoke very little English—now that was a process, finding the number of a veterinarian in the phone book. When I actually dialed the number, he answered the phone! I was flabbergasted. What animal clinic in America can you call and actually talk to the veterinarian who is waiting for you when you arrive? The office visit, flea medication for all four dogs, an antibiotic shot for Woody along with some oral medicine, came to a grand total of just under $30. Can you believe it? Dr. Gonzalez also prescribed fresh papaya blended with milk, and mineral oil. He explained that Woody has swollen glands and, since dogs can't cough, they throw up any drainage in their throat. Woody will get another shot of antibiotics tomorrow and a final one on Friday. Wow, the service here is incredible.

Boot camp starts tomorrow at 8 a.m.—a warm-up beside the pool, a run on the beach, and then back to the pool area to finish up with calisthenics and abdominal crunches. A one-hour workout after the run! Yikes!

Chapter 7 – Boot Camp Day 1

I survived my first day of boot camp with a smile (grimace) on my face. After the workout we went back to the vet to get Woody another shot, to the health club to check out the schedule, and then the Wednesday market that is held in downtown Guaymas. It is a huge outdoor market and we were only able to cover about a third of it but I still managed to find three funky skirts for under $7. After all the shopping we were famished, so of course we had to go out for a delicious lunch of grilled pollo and ensalada.

We then came home and I tried to prepare for my first Spanish lesson when I hit the wall! Brain dead, unable to make a sentence, comatose! So instead of a lesson, Francisco, my tutor, took one look at me and made another plan. Starting Tuesday, he will come over one hour a day for five days, and we'll see how that works out. Since I don't have much Spanish background, it should be a challenge. He has a great attitude and said we would have fun! Did I mention he is adorable?

And the real reason I'm so tired is the diet—meat and salad. No sugar or carbs, no booze, no caffeine. I always get tired for the first few days of any diet and then I feel great.

My legs are sore from the workout and we're doing it again early tomorrow morning.

So that's it for the Silly Woman diary tonight. I'm in bed, exhausted and it's only 7 p.m.!

Chapter 8 – A Nose Waxing?

Boot camp Day 2. Jeezzzz, were my legs sore this morning! And, we worked them again today. After our morning run we ran in place by the pool, did some jumping up and down, and side to side like boxers do (not sure how I know THAT), and more abdominal crunches—a one-hour workout. So far, so good with no booze, caffeine or carbs. The weariness has gone away and been replaced with super energy. Now if the legs would cooperate I would be in business. They are okay for walking; it's when I try to sit down or bend over that it hurts like hell! It's a good thing. . . I think.

After all that work, it was time for some pampering at the nail spa. I had my face waxed, starting with the brows and moving down to the NOSE. Can you believe it? They actually waxed my nose—and not the inside. Some people get their crotch waxed but Oh No, not me. I go for the nose wax. I had no clue there was any hair on it but she showed me the proof. Weird. But now my nose, along with the rest of my face, is soft as a baby's butt. The face buzz and a French manicure was a grand total of $17.50. The dollar is at 1.4! It's like everything's on sale. I continue to live large on my Wal-Mart budget.

The weather is balmy, the men are handsome, and the price is right. Can it get any better than this?

Chapter 9 – Poor Woody

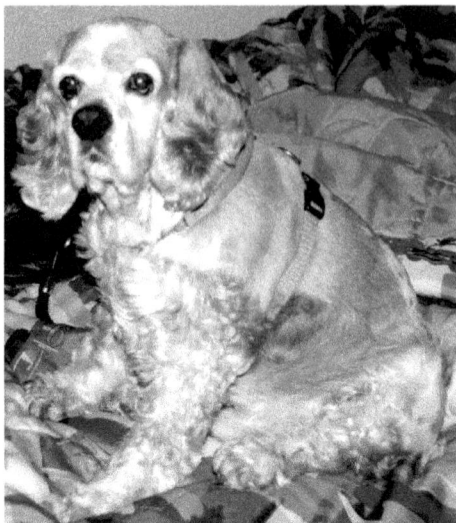

I awake at 5:30 a.m. to the sound of retching again. The familiar sound that I know to be Woody. His little body lurching forward a few times before the vomit comes. I rush him outside and he lays down three piles of last night's dinner, complete with undigested peas in green slime—I know, this is way too much information, but this IS how my day started. After a few more trips outside we manage to get him settled down and he even opted to eat his breakfast of yogurt. By now you can guess what time it is—the start of day 3 boot camp. I'm off to the beach with the dogs to do my one-mile run (still walking and running, BTW), hoping that Woody will hold his own, or actually not minding the thought of stopping if he gets sick again. My legs are stiff but actually feel better than they did yesterday morning. Woody is better and actually never had to pause for a puke break.

There are many more dead birds in the surf today, including babies. They are both beautiful and tragic to look at. I made a mental note to contact the World Wildlife Federation in San Carlos to find out exactly why these birds are dying. I've been hearing that this is a much larger problem on the West Coast for pelicans. Many are dying. . . but why?

The tide is almost entirely in, so running on the beach is difficult, at best, but somehow we get through it and find our way back to the house, just as the sun starts getting really warm. We gather around the salt-water solar pool and begin our routine. Antonio, the boot camp guru switched it up today, giving us somewhat of a break, or so it seems. We did arm presses, and triceps work without the weights. And, our jogging, jumping jacks and pushups seemed easier. Did we actually do less, or am I getting used to it? We count in Spanish so it's hard for me to tell, but I am learning: uno, dos, tres, cuatro, etc. It's when we get in the teens that I get lost. We finished with the killer abs crunches again, both bad and good. Bad because it hurts like hell, and good because we know we have almost completed another day of boot camp and survived!

I called Dr. Gonzales in San Carlos again, thinking I should take Woody back in, since it is the start of a weekend. He said my little doggie just needs some time, and that he is available 24-7 in the event I need to call him this weekend. He even makes house calls. I could really get used to this service.

So, I have elected to stay home today with the dogs and lay in the sun—I know you're not suppose to do that anymore, but I never did like rules. So with my sugarless limeade, a novel, and my Hawaiian tanning oil (SPF 4, did you know it's really hard to find oil without sunscreen anymore?), I am set for a day of sunbathing and cooling off in the pool. After sitting in the pool—which is great for the muscles in my legs— I returned to my chair to find Zippy stretched out on my pink towel, with my sunglasses and book nearby. It was obviously a photo op. She is such a hoot. It's hard to ever be mad around her, although she can be extremely trying at times, especially when she wants to run in the opposite direction, pulling me backwards as I try to run forward. As if running isn't hard enough for me anyway. . .

So tonight is my "coming-out" party in Guaymas. More later. . . on that event.

Chapter 10 - Coming-Out Party

The coming-out event last night turned out to be a dinner party of about 10 people. Since Juanita had a commitment this weekend, we decided to postpone the large dancing party that will include many of the local Mexican people, until mid-February, when my neighbor Margaret, from the wedding-gown fiasco, arrives from Vashon. We picked up the food from Antonio's brother, who does catering on the side. Beef, beans, and handmade tortillas with all the condiments was $15, but that's only $1.50 each and we had mucho leftovers! It looked absolutely delicious—although in sticking with the weekly diet plan, the only thing I ate was beef with salsa on top and a green salad.

The people here were Americans living in San Carlos, a very nice gringo town about 15 minutes away. John and Connie have lived here part of the time for over 30 years, returning to their home state of Utah for the Sonora summers. Dave and Meryl have owned a home here for a few years. They brought two friends with them; Sharon is visiting from Boise, and Sabine from Italy is married to a Frenchman and they split their time between Boise and Europe. Meryl and Dave are retired school teacher/principal and spend their time between

San Carlos and Boise. Tammy arrived with a bottle of Australian wine that she got at Costco in Hermosillo, about an hour north of here. She is a real estate agent living with Miguel, a well-connected local real estate developer.

It was relaxing just sitting around getting to know everyone. However, not one of them knew what was killing the pelicans on the beach. Apparently, it is a problem all over the West Coast. I will find the WWF next week in search of answers. In the meantime, I am fascinated with photographing these beautiful creatures.

So okay, if you MUST know, Silly Woman had two drinks of tequila—mixed with bubbly lime mineral water. It's on the diet, and NO, the wine was not. Weird I don't even feel like wine in this weather. But, back to the drinks. . .it wasn't a margarita but it wasn't bad, either. This morning I could feel it. Interesting that I haven't drank in a few weeks, and I was able to feel the effects of just two drinks. I don't know what it all means other than just an observation. Don't panic, I'm not ready to swear off booze just yet.

So today the doggies and I are alone at Casa Miramar. The weekend is a reprieve from boot camp, but I still did my morning run and some yoga stretches. The soreness has turned into only an awareness of the muscles. I am reading a book written about Guaymas and the red-light district in the '70s called "Zone of Tolerance" by David Stuart. The book has my attention for the moment as I sit in the lounge chair by the pool. The breeze makes sitting in the sun very pleasant. My body craves the Vitamin D that I miss in the Alaska winters, so I am taking full advantage of soaking up the rays.

A couple of observations: the beach is cluttered with bottles and cans in the morning. What I learned from the locals was that the cans are purposely left on the beach so that the poorer residents can collect them and redeem them for cash. The other insight was that food here is extremely bland—very good, but no spices. When you order chicken, steak or seafood, it comes plain with little seasonings. So that's it, all the insights for today.

And in case you are wondering. . . Woody is back to his old self today. Like Dr. Gonzalez said, he just needed more time to get the bacteria out of his system.

Chapter 11 – Embracing the Culture, ALONE

The realization that I am indeed in a foreign country slapped me in the face today. When I travel, I am conscientious about embracing cultural differences, but sometimes I forget and assume, and find myself being jolted back into the reality of the moment, like today.

I needed some things at the grocery, so I went to my favorite neighborhood store in San Carlos—a small space with lots of fresh fruits and vegetables. Of course, the whole of San Carlos is made up of gringos, so language is not a problem. I grabbed the main stuff to continue my protein diet when I realized there was no lettuce on the shelves. That is one of very few staples on my current diet plan, so I have to have it. This meant I would have to go to the BIG store in Guaymas (the working-class town where everyone speaks Spanish)—alone.

Finding my way to downtown Guaymas was easy and I was feeling pretty confident when I pulled into the parking lot. I could not believe how many people were there! It was then that I realized this super-store was smack in the middle of the city center mall, and the people were out en masse. After all, it is Sunday afternoon. I have only been to downtown

Guaymas with Juanita at my side to speak for me. I've been listening to Mexican radio in hopes that subliminally it will soak into my brain and I will magically start speaking fluent Spanish. So far, it's not working.

Supermercado Ley has everything available for purchase that you can imagine—exactly the type of American store that I avoid at all costs. I actually hyperventilate when I get in this type of shopping frenzy. So my plan was to run in, grab the lettuce, pay for it and get the hell out. The first problem was finding it, for a quick in-and-out. Not possible. Especially when I was unable to ask directions.

I could not understand what was going on around me, nor did I have a clue as to where the produce was located. But I was obviously in the middle of a friendly, relaxed, slow-moving crowd. It's all about the adventure, right? I was on one end of the grocery section, the lettuce was on the total opposite side of the store, or so I found out after meandering around for what seemed like forever. Finally, I got what I needed and headed to the checkout. Where might that be? Another bout of wandering around until I accidentally stumbled onto the checkout isles. Did I mention the hordes of people? OMG.

I had the lettuce and was knee deep in a line behind folks

that had multiple carts of food to check. I glanced around to find the 10-items-or-less line, but no one had less than 10 things but me. I was in for the duration and decided to enjoy the present moment as it was presented to me. Crying babies, women chatting, teenage boys reading Hustler magazine—in fact, everyone was reading magazines off the shelf. The man behind me was trying to talk to me and I was replying with the one phrase that I do know, *"non español,"* and flashing him a big smile. He just continued talking, saying who knows what?

My observation? Ok, as a people-watcher, it IS about what you see. People ARE happy here. No one appeared in a rush, impatient or angry. Everyone is smiling and polite. And in the midst of all this chaos, I managed to get my stuff checked out without having to speak one word. Muchas gracias.

I am starting Spanish lessons on Tuesday and want to learn some basic phrases. It's going to be memorizing and learning verbs. Motivation comes when you realize you don't have a clue what people are saying, or how to ask for anything. When I do try to speak, it always comes out in French and people look at me weird, especially the waiter, who asked me a question and I responded with "oui." I haven't greeted anyone with a bonjour yet.

Tomorrow is weigh-in, another tummy-laser zap, and a different diet plan for the week! We are back to boot camp first thing in the morning. Tonight I'm listening to the Doors "Break On Through" on Mexican radio—it must be gringo night. Something I CAN understand!

Chapter 12 – Monday Weigh-In

Weigh-in was today at 11:30 a.m. at the diet center. On the way there we told ourselves it was okay if we hadn't lost any weight for the week. But the good news is Juanita and I both lost 1.5 kilos—which computes to 3.3 pounds each. I already feel lighter, and when you visualize what 3.3 pounds of raw hamburger looks like, well, that's how much has fallen off my body in one week. But, the best part—I'm not even hungry and I don't crave anything.

For the record, during week one I could eat: cereal with light milk, toast with light marmalade, fresh-squeezed OJ available here (yummy), meat (no pork, shrimp or shellfish), chicken, fish and salad, plus jicama for a snack (tastes great dipped in salsa). Well, week two is a little more restrictive: eggs, ham, bacon, OJ, light Jell-O, tuna, chicken, one piece of fruit per day (no grapes or mango), beef and salad. This is easy to remember and different enough from last week to keep it interesting.

Along with new menus we also had our acupressure and tummy-laser zaps. The acupressure points are located by the right ear on the jaw, with mouth open, and on the shoulder near the collarbone (same side). That must be the magic that takes the appetite away. The old laser tape was removed from the stomach, replaced with new strips and zapped. And did I mention this cost is only $6? We celebrated by going out to lunch at a downtown hotel but, motivated by the weight loss, we stuck to our diet plan.

Still puzzled by the dead birds on the beach, we made a concerted effort to find the World Wildlife Federation in downtown Guaymas after lunch. We were directed to several buildings before learning that the local office had moved to Hermosillo, the capital of Sonora, about three hours north of here. I guess any future investigation into the deaths of these birds will have to be done online. I already read that it was indeed a mystery on the West Coast and, to date, only one scientist had a theory about climate change as a possible reason for their demise.

Well, another reprieve from boot camp—Antonio had the day off, so we start again tomorrow at 8 a.m. He mentioned that we were going to do trail running this week. I think that means uphill. SHIT! I ran this morning on the beach and told Zippy she could come along IF she promised to run in the same direction as me. She agreed and did pretty well. Yesterday, I could hear her howling from across the street because I had left her behind. That's one way to meet the neighbors.

After my run, I went to yoga at the health club in San Carlos to see what they were offering. Although the sign said Beginners Level, it was so NOT beginners. We started out doing balancing poses and people were weaving and falling all over the place. It renewed my inspiration to get a routine together so that I can volunteer at the club for the eight hours needed for certification. A few more observations that I have to write down or I will definitely forget:

Ordering a salad in a restaurant means iceberg lettuce.

Women wear false eyelashes like we did in the '70s—well, some of us.

Women do not wear shorts.

Women wear skin-tight stretch jeans. A young lady walked by our table in a pair and Juanita said it reminded her of a "sausage." You know, like sausage meat pressed into those skins? OMG—now THAT was funny!

High heels—with the tight jeans comes the stilettos—how do women walk in them?

American women are easy to spot.

There are many spirits in Guaymas. There was one sitting in the backseat of the car today.

Chapter 13 – Back to Basics

Back to boot camp at 8 a.m. this morning. I can sure tell I had three days off, even though I ran and did yoga stretches over the weekend. It's interesting that Antonio uses free weights and basic calisthenics in our workout. His experience comes from military training, so we work mostly on strength and endurance, toning in the process.

Long before the health club rage, this was how people stayed in shape. These exercises are so basic, yet challenging and effective. The abdominal crunches at the end are a killer, but they are the sign that we're almost through for another day. Antonio's brother-in-law is a professional boxer and he told us about some cream to apply on our fat spots to reduce it? Supposedly, it makes you sweat profusely in the specific areas applied. Boxers swear by it, so we had to have it. It smells like menthol, looks like and has the consistency of lemon curd, but it's worth a try, right?

Since I am working so hard at this, I deserve a treat and it can't be chocolate. So after boot camp, I drive to the nail salon for a relaxing, manual manicure. I'm really into orange lately, so orange toes and fingertips it is.

Chapter 14 - "Juanita, Juanita, Zippy!"

This morning I was again reminded that OgDog would not be with me forever. Last night he peed his bed and was lying in it, seemingly unaware. This is only one of several subtle changes that have occurred lately. When a dog reaches the elderly years, change is expected but it is still a shock when it happens. It is the life process and I do my best to make him comfortable. And, if we need to get some Depends, so be it.

He still LOVES to eat and all working parts are functioning, as they should. He's an amazing guy; every time I count him out, he rebounds stronger than ever. And, he loves lying in the Mexican sunshine almost as much as I do.

But the real chronicle of the day is Zippy. The dogs and I went to the beach for our evening walk with Zippy on leash. I've been feeling sorry for her lately because the others are free to roam around and she's not; however, they DO listen and stay close to me. I let her off last night and she did great, so once again I unhooked the leash and she took off running in the sand. The houses are built near the ocean and the walls are connected, so there are only a few places to get back to the street. She was doing great, enjoying all the dogs and people on the beach, coming back to me when I called her, doing what she should do to remain a free dog.

We walked about half a mile down the beach and then turned around and headed back. It was during this little roundabout that Zippy disappeared. She was there, and then, presto, GONE! Apparently, she found an opening to the street and the beach walk was not holding her interest. She needed to be where people pay attention to her, and only her—and where begging for food has real potential. She prefers an outdoor restaurant to a boring beach walk any day.

This is not the first time she has escaped and ran around the neighborhood, so I was determined to teach her a lesson and not go looking for her like I usually do. Let her find her own way home, I'm tired of this game. The other dogs and I headed back to the house, but on the way I notice another beautiful dead bird that I wanted to photograph before dark. I took the spaniel's home, grabbed my camera and headed back across the street to the beach—still no sign of Zippy. She can be exasperating at times!

I photographed the pelican and starting talking with a guy and his dog on the beach. The sun was sinking below the horizon and I was beginning to get worried, so I mentioned my dog had run off and asked if he had seen her. He said that he had seen a "Hush Puppy" dog about three blocks away, and had to stop his car to let her cross the street—say no more, of course, this is ZipDog. He also told me she was a very nice dog and I should get her right away because someone might steal her. Oh, great!

Back to the house to drop off the camera, open the gate, get my car keys and go looking for the silly dog. I drove up the street a few blocks, and nothing. There were two men working on a car, so I stopped to ask if they had seen her. They responded in Spanish and were waving and pointing toward the beach, and I couldn't understand any of it.

I rushed back to the house—by the way, it is now dark—to get Juanita to translate. She got in the car, we rolled the windows down and are yelling "*Zippy*" all the way back to the men and their car. They tell Juanita that the dog was running back to the beach the last time they saw her. We turn around and drive very slowly yelling for her out the windows. I saw headlights in my rear-view mirror and pulled over so that the car could pass, when suddenly we heard honking and shouting from an SUV that pulled up behind us – "*Juanita! Juanita!*"

Chaos ensued as I stopped the car. Juanita jumped out, and they were speaking what sounded to me like frantic Spanish (multiple voices) and I'm just trying to get someone to tell me what's going on. I finally heard "*Juanita, Juanita, Zippy*" (that's all I could understand), and then Juanita says "*Zippy!*" in a surprised tone. I got out of the car at this point and, sure enough, there she was in their SUV. I cannot believe this dog. She will get in the car with anyone. These Mexican guys were so great; in fact, many neighbors on the street were engaged in the search. Can you imagine? And, of course, DoDog loved the attention. I kissed these guys on the cheek and said muchas gracias a dozen times. Juanita decided to walk home (smart woman) and I'm finally on my way home to relax. NOT!

Zippy got in VeVe and we headed home when I quickly noticed a gross odor permeating the air, coming from the backseat. OMG, she had rolled in something so nasty that I could hardly breathe during the short ride back to the house. That's it, now I have to give the damn dog a shower before she can stay in the house. We came in the front door and I was scolding her; the spaniels are running for cover but are also extremely interested in the "smell."

GAWD! I could not get her in the shower quick enough, turned it on full blast and went to get the shampoo, while she slipped out of the bathroom. Now I am chasing a wet basset hound around the casita, slipping on the tiled floor because I'm wet and so is she. I cannot believe I am wrestling a 40-pound hound dog to the ground and then carrying her back to the bathroom. I finally got her back in the shower, lathered up and rinsed twice, just to be sure the smell was gone. I am completely soaked from head to toe by now because I was in the shower with all my clothes on. I dried her off, shut her in the bathroom, got out of the wet clothes and into my cozy bathrobe just as Juanita poked her head in and said, *"You need a drink?"* And Silly Woman didn't even hesitate, vodka please.

Later, in a vodka-induced trance, I went to sleep only to dream about car horns blowing and an SUV full of guys shouting, *"Juanita, Juanita, Zippy."* What a great neighborhood. What a funny dog. She has an innate way of bringing people together, even when she stinks!

Chapter 15 – Market Day

The boot camp continues and, just when I start to get comfortable with the routine, the intensity increases. My body is no longer as "sore" as it is fatigued. It's an awareness I feel in the different areas I work, especially the ones needing it the most. I lather myself up with the boxer cream every morning, put on my sweatshirt and go to the beach for a run, in hopes of sweating off some fat. Antonio actually had on four shirts today and they were soaked, so it seems to work. My body may be fatigued but my energy level is amazing. I went to bed at 1 a.m. after the shower fiasco with ZipDog, and woke up at 7 a.m., ready to go.

Today is Wednesday—market day in downtown Guaymas. You can buy anything from fresh fruits and vegetables to clothing, furniture, electronics and flowers. You name it. The streets are closed off and the vendors display their wares from 9-2. Bartering is the game, but the prices are already so extremely low that I don't bother much. The goal today was to get Zippy a bikini. Juanita found her the perfect pink/green polo suit that will look great once we cut a hole out for her tail. She was so proud when we put it on her. But now Luce's nose is out of joint because she didn't get one.

Marti gras carnival is next week in Guaymas, so we were looking for costumes. I found a very colorful, somewhat racy dress (backless, low-cut neckline, and tight on the body) and will go the fabric store sometime before Monday to find a mask. Handmade masks are everywhere. The carnival starts on Monday and lasts all week—singing, dancing, eating, and entertainment. I love the way the Mexicans celebrate. It's too much fun. And Margaret, my neighbor from Vashon (who becomes Maggie in Mexico), arrives on Monday! What is it about the name changes? Is this the alter ego coming out? Or could it be the id?

After market, we went out to lunch and I had planta—barbecue grilled white fish that had the consistency of halibut, with steamed vegetables and a lemonada. Perfect! After a short siesta, we headed to the heath club for a much-appreciated Jacuzzi— Ahhhhh. . . it felt fabulous on the body. We checked on tennis lessons and realized we have to buy racquets before we can start—one more thing to add to a long list of things to do.

We stopped at Dave and Meryl's (she is called Jasmine in Mexico) on the way home. They have a lovely house in San Carlos. We made a date tomorrow to go to La Manga, a fishing village near here that uses a generator for power. They are known for their fresh seafood. We are also planning on hiking a mountain in lieu of boot camp on Friday. Antonio said we would run it. I have a feeling I'm in for the extreme running challenge, and everyone knows I'm NOT a runner. But I will remain open to the challenge. Yikes!

Chapter 16 - La Manga

Boot camp was the usual today. We are hiking Mount Teta Kawi tomorrow to end the week. Sounds like a good way to break up the routine, or so I thought tonight. I'm back to dog chasing today. Zippy escaped AGAIN while Antonio was speaking to the carpenter at the entrance gate. She just quietly slipped by him. When I went looking for her in the yard it was apparent that Houdini has once again hit the streets. Antonio headed in one direction, and I got in the car with a leash to go the other way. I see the wonderful man who helped me last night. I show him the empty leash and he pointed to his eye and then to the alley behind the street—by now he knows I don't speak much Spanish so he resorted to sign language, all the while shaking his head. I parked the car and followed him through a vacant lot and there was Zippy, shoulder to shoulder with a tall, thin street dog that she had befriended, sashaying down the alley, both of them grinning from ear-to-ear. She runs free in her Homer neighborhood and can't seem to grasp that it is not acceptable behavior in Mexico.

Dinner tonight was in the fishing village of La Manga, which, incidentally, reminds me of an Alaskan native village. The natives here are part of the Seri tribe that was

50

dislocated because of development in the area. Years ago they were apparently shunned by the Mexican government because of alleged cannibalism. The people at La Manga were friendly and we had a great meal of fillet of fish (I think), smothered in garlic, along with a salad. This village has no electricity, so everything was on a generator. The outdoor restaurant sits on a cliff and overlooks the Sea of Cortez. It closed at sunset, which was absolutely incredible tonight. I don't usually photograph sunsets because they never look as spectacular in a picture as they really are, but bear with me, I WAS inspired here. Dave, Jasmine, Gail, Juanita and I acted like the tourists we really are, snapping shot after shot as the sky continued changing, until the sun sank below the horizon.

We headed back to San Carlos and stopped at an art gallery having an opening. Three artists from Tucson were displaying their work. I met Mark McMahon, a prior dentist who had cashed in his lucrative practice to drive to Ushuaia, Tierra del Fuego, Argentina, the southernmost city in the world. A photographer and writer now, I bought his book detailing his adventure: "Driving to the End of the World."

I also met Chandika Tazouz, an artist who has spent time in Alaska traveling the festivals and selling her artwork. She knows and loves Homer. She told me that she was so broke at one point that she became a dancer for two months. Apparently, I didn't get what she was telling me because she further explained she was a dancing stripper! And that she made tons of money because some of the men preferred the older women (she's about 65 now) to the young ones. Hilarious!

Back in the car and headed home, Jasmine suggested that since I have not been to Froggies yet, and it is a must see by gringo standards, we needed to go. Okay, so Dave said he wanted to be dropped off at the house, gave Jasmine 500 pesos, which amounts to about $50, and sent us on our way to the bar. Did he think we were going to drink all night and pick up men? Juanita found an illegal parking spot near the entrance and, as we were getting out of the car, a man pulled up and told her firmly that we could not park there because he needed to get past us into his driveway. BTW, everyone speaks English here. Juanita got out, flashed him a big smile and told him that she thought he had plenty of room to get by. He commented that if she didn't have such a nice smile, he would never go for this, but if we would help direct him past our van, then we could stay parked there. As it turned out, Juanita was right, he had plenty of room! We all shouted muchas gracias as he squeezed past our parked vehicle that was blocking his driveway.

As we entered the bar, I was back home again. Froggies looks like an Alaskan bar, similar to the Salty Dawg in Homer. Smoking, '80s music (I've heard more Jimmy Morrison in Mexico than I have heard in years!), karaoke, T-shirts hanging from the ceiling, drunk gringos hitting on women—you know the drill. Juanita and I had one drink and headed home. Jasmine and Gail are on their own if they want to stay longer. Of course, Jasmine's house is within walking distance of the bar. I can now add Froggies to my list of bars in San Carlos, but I don't feel the need to return anytime soon. I much prefer the bars where I can't understand what's going on around me—although I have yet to go to one. There's always mañana!

Chapter 17 – The Crud

The Silly Woman diary entry for today is rather uneventful as I spent the day in bed with the crud—I woke up last night about three times feeling like I was going to be sick. I managed to go back to sleep without that happening, but when I got up this morning to prepare for the boot camp mountain climb/run, I realized there was no way I could do it—nauseated, diarrhea, achy, exhausted . . . I think I hit the wall. So okay, I'm a weenie for not making the hike today, but when Margaret gets here next week we will definitely have to do it.

In the meantime, I'm spending time in the bathroom, lying in the sun, in the bathroom, in the bed, in the bathroom, back to the bed. I cannot eat anything, including water—it comes right back up. And I keep thinking of that garlic and butter that was on the fish last night. You know if we listen to our bodies we can figure out the problem. My diet has been bland for over two weeks; so all of that extreme richness has to pass through my system before I will actually feel better.

When Juanita got home from the mountain run that I obviously missed, she suggested I eat a saltine cracker and suck on ice cubes. A few hours after keeping that down, she made me toast with marmalade, the best toast ever. So I'm watching movies and being pampered. The dogs are concerned and beside me on the bed all day. Who could ask for better companions when I feel like shit?

And the good news is, I know I will be better mañana!

Chapter 18 - Valentine's Day

Another day spent recuperating. Although I feel so much better than yesterday, my stomach is still a bit queasy. The dogs and I ran this morning and then retired to the back deck for some much-needed Vitamin D sunshine and a good book. Did I mention I'm hooked on watching the beginning ER series on DVD, with George Clooney? That's what staying in bed for a day will do for you.

Interesting, I have lost my appetite entirely and think it has to be the acupressure, which is a good thing. Just the thought of food turns my stomach—so okay, I'm not completely over the crud. But the upshot is this will definitely help take off some unwanted pounds. We'll see how Monday weigh-in goes with the diet doctor.

This afternoon we went to San Carlos in search of bellybutton jewelry. I have an appointment with a doctor in Guaymas on Tuesday to get it pierced. Yikes! No luck in finding anything so will have to go back to the Supermercado Ley shopping center in the city to get the sterilized post. I'm a little nervous as I had it pierced once before and it never quite healed. Everything around my waist seemed to constantly irritate it, so after about six weeks I got fed up and took out the hoop and threw it away. Being in Mexico means wearing fewer clothes than Alaska (really?), so I'm hoping this time it will heal really fast with the help of loose clothing and lots of sun.

It's Valentine's Day and there are festivals all around. I heard that it's a bigger holiday here than in the States—the Mexicans are romantic people and love parties. On Valentine's Eve there was music down the street for most of the night. They were having so much fun. When I got up this morning Juanita told me she had once again gone dancing without me. Can you believe it? The music woke her up around 12, so she got up, dressed up, and went to the party! At least she didn't wear her bathrobe like last time. I can't believe she didn't get me up. But, I was still recuperating from a long day in bed. One night it will be ME that gets up, and heads down the street toward the loud music and dancing crowd! And knowing Juanita, she will already be there.

Chapter 19 – Another Weigh-In

Monday morning, weigh-in day—I'm up early, so the dogs and I head to the beach for our usual run. It's overcast and a little chilly this morning, but I'm not complaining. It's still warmer than Alaska. I see Antonio has arrived, so I hurry and feed the dogs, as boot camp is about to start. About this time Juanita comes to my back door and announces that Antonio said we're taking the day off! He thinks we have been working really hard and eating very little, so it's time for a rest. Fine by me. I'm not complaining about that either!

Our most exciting task for today is going to the diet center to see how much weight we have lost, and get a new menu for the week. I was surprised to learn that I had dropped another 3.5 pounds. So the total for two weeks is about 7 pounds. Juanita has lost approximately 14 pounds in four weeks. So for week three my choices are: cereal, plain yogurt with fruit (anything but mangos, grapes and bananas), vegetable soup, chicken, fish, and jicama with salsa, salad and lots of water. I'm going to miss that fresh-squeezed OJ every morning. The diet doctor, who is really a nutritionist that does acupressure, zapped our tummy fat with a laser and stimulated the two pressure points that will suppress our appetites for another week.

Good news means now it's time to celebrate, but first we have to shop for our carnival masks. The fabric store has a zillion hand-painted masks and both of us select several, plus we found these wonderful cowboy hats that are covered in glitter. Juanita got a lime green one, and mine is a brilliant blue. The festivities begin on Thursday night and go through Fat Tuesday. Lots of parades, the crowning of a king and queen, dancing on the square, carnival rides and who knows what else?

Juanita told me that she's feeling goofy and her vision was blurry (low blood sugar), so it is definitely time for some food. We went to La Botono's for lunch and I ordered pollo fajitas. Since we are both losing weight, we decided we could "cheat" a bit today. We took four tortilla chips each and broke them up into tiny pieces and dipped them in salsa. Remember the book "French Women Don't Get Fat"? The theory is you can satisfy any food urge with only four bites. After eating four broken-up chips (okay, so it was more than four bites), the urge had actually passed. Amazing. . .

When we got home there was a phone message inviting us out to dinner with a group of friends—back to La Botono's tonight for another plate of pollo fajitas. I haven't eaten this much in days, and it's all food on my diet, and delicious! The city was alive with people setting up for the carnival. After dinner, we walked around the city streets, to the fountain, and back through the square, ending another fun-filled busy day. They just seem to fly by!

Oh, on my way to bed I realized Zippy was still outside in the yard. I called her and then walked around the house just as she ran past me, swiping my leg with a wet body. Now, WHY is she wet? After further investigation, I think I know what happened. Antonio put the cover on the pool today so that it would warm up quicker, and apparently Zippy thought she could walk on it, which of course means she fell in the pool. Obviously, she had quite a struggle, based on the amount of water on the patio. It actually looked like someone had done a belly flop into the water. Poor girl, she must have been pretty frightened out there all alone, fighting to get out of the water. She was certainly in a hurry to get in the house and went straight to the bathroom to get toweled off. She is now snuggled under the covers, fast asleep.

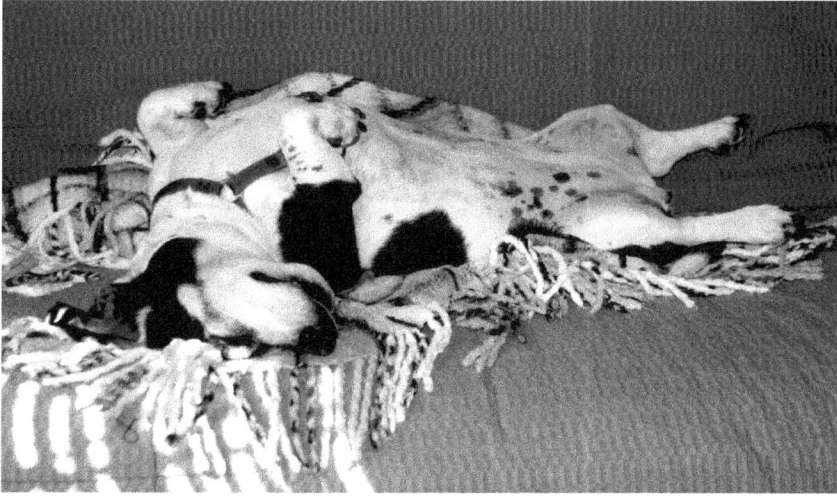

So now we're home in bed at 8 p.m. because we have to get up in only five hours to pick up Margaret, the Vashon neighbor (soon to be Maggie) at the bus terminal at 1:40 a.m. We decided to do it carnival-style to see if she recognized us— bathrobes, masks and glittered cowboy hats. What is it about going out at night in bathrobes here?

Chapter 20 – Cowboy Hats & Bathrobes

Today was the ultimate abdominal toner. When I finally went to bed, my sides and tummy were aching from laughing my ass off! It began at 1 a.m. when Juanita and I got out of bed to pick up Margaret (soon to be Maggie) at the bus station. We set the internal clock so that we would have time to get in full carnival attire before leaving: masks, bathrobes and cowboy hats, all color coordinated. The first problem was getting Juanita in the driver's seat with her hat; it was bumping the roof of the van and causing her mask to slide down over her eyes. Not good—especially for the driver. I finally agreed that it was okay to leave her hat off until we got to the station.

We arrived with only a few minutes to spare and were surprised to see so many people, both inside and out. As we got out of the car, Juanita felt the need to explain how we looked to everyone. *"Ah, carnival, si?"* And they all agreed. People were laughing, opening doors for us and probably thinking we were nuts. It was the bathrobes that drew the most attention.

We found some seats on the back row and waited as the bus pulled in. When Margaret (almost Maggie) passed through the door, she saw us immediately (who could miss us?) and of course burst out laughing, causing us to collapse into a fit of giggles, tears streaming down our faces. Several people in the crowd got caught up in our reunion, and they too were laughing.

Back to the casa by 2:30 a.m., we unloaded the car outside the gate and were showing Maggie (she's now in Guaymas, so the name change is effective) around when the doorbell rang. The three of us froze, looking at each other and wondering WTF? After much debate, we finally opened the gate to find two uniformed police officers wanting to know if everything was OK. Apparently, during all the excitement we had left the car doors and the back hatch, wide open with the keys dangling in the ignition! The patrolmen cruising the neighborhood thought it looked very suspicious. It's good to know we live in a safe neighborhood. Relieved and giddy, we hugged the officers saying muchas gracias over and over! They pulled away from Casa Miramar laughing and shaking their heads at 3 Silly Women, 2 of them in bathrobes and cowboy hats, and the other one looking like a typical American tourist.

We continued our reunion making carnival plans, eventually retiring for a few hours sleep before . . . Maggie's first day of boot camp!

Chapter 21 – Seven Pounds Lighter

At 9 a.m. Maggie was officially inducted into our boot camp routine (although Antonio took it easy on us because she was new), followed by my first private Spanish lesson. So much information to comprehend, some confusing, some not—my brain is on overload after one hour. It was over just at the time I thought I couldn't think anymore. Francisco did say I had a natural accent—not sure I believe him, but it was good to hear anyhow.

It is now time for a break, so I'm off to the Santa Rosa market with Maggie, and an idea. I am a visual person so I need to SEE what seven pounds actually looks like to understand how much of me has disappeared in the last two weeks. I told the butcher I needed seven kilos of hamburger meat. He looked at me a little weird and began stacking up beef, more beef and then more beef, to run through the grinder. I told Maggie that it sure looked like a lot and she asked me how much weight I had lost. I then realized what I had ordered and, fortunately, was able to stop him before he ground up the entire 15 pounds. What I really needed to equal seven pounds was three kilos – Silly Woman.

I was excited to get back to the casa with my beef. I

arranged it on a beautiful green ceramic cake plate and took some pictures. When I looked at seven pounds of hamburger meat and equated that to being what came off of my body, it was really gross—and, of course, very funny. Especially when we tried to lift the meat sculpture and hold it overhead for the photo op. Juanita has lost twice this much—can you imagine? We also thought about using butter—that would be 28 sticks of butter for me, and 56 for Juanita. After this exercise, we see weight loss in a whole different perspective—and may never eat hamburger or butter again.

Chapter 22 – The Piercing Surgeon

By now it's time for my 4 o'clock appointment with Dr. Ruiz for my bellybutton piercing—a referral from the nail salon. We arrived at his office a few minutes early; of course, no one has a watch, and the sign said closed until 4. We meander up the block doing some window-shopping when this bright red car with chrome wheels rounds the corner.

A man with a shaved head, donning dark glasses, slams on his brakes, backs up a few feet, rolls his window down and shouts at us over the street traffic: *"Are you here for a piercing?"* I'm stunned, so Juanita says, *"si,"* as he guns the engine and pulls into the parking lot of the office. Is this the doctor? How do you suppose he knew we were waiting for him when we're not even near his office? Do I have a sign on my forehead that says, *"Pierce me"* or WHAT? Now I'm nervous.

We entered the waiting room in hysterics, as he disappeared behind closed doors for a few minutes. He reappeared and invited me inside, but told Maggie and Juanita to wait. He's nicely dressed, has a hint of cologne, and is actually pretty handsome. It turns out he's a surgeon at the hospital, but does body piercing in his private office. Okay, so I sit on a table high enough to put him eye level with my belly, which he said is beautiful. Did I mention how nervous I was? Well, to be honest, I was a wreck! I did this piercing thing once before at a tattoo studio in West Virginia, and it hurt like hell.

Juanita and Maggie asked through the wall if I'm okay—and I told them so far so good. I held my breath and looked straight ahead, refusing to look down to see what's going on for fear of the pain. He gave me a quick shot of Lidocaine and proceeded to complete the piercing before I even realized it was over. This was a walk in the park. I couldn't believe he was finished!

He was part Italian and extremely flirtatious—now that explains the flamboyancy. Juanita was summoned to come into the exam room to interpret when we got into "Spanglish" (his word, when he couldn't understand what I was asking). The Lidocaine wore off hours later and I had absolutely NO pain in my bellybutton, and the piercing cost all of $10.

The whole experience was so funny. I often felt like I was in a Hollywood movie in Mexico. Bizarre, crazy scenarios just kept happening. I made another appointment with Dr. Ruiz to get my ears re-pierced just so I could take my camera and photograph him in his red car! And, of course, it has nothing to do with the fact he is adorable.

This is the end of another truly hilarious day. And we're not even drinking, and carnival doesn't start until Thursday. If this continues, there won't be a need for any abdominal work; my stomach stays sore enough from laughing my ass off daily.

Chapter 23 – Spirits in the Casa

We had the killer leg workout this morning. My legs are already stiff, so that means tomorrow will be tough. So much for a break because of Maggie—she's no longer a newbie. Antonio is training us on endurance, strength and repetition, and is picking up the pace. In the middle of a difficult repetition, I reminded the girls that we should think about the shopping we would be doing in a few hours, instead of the pain!

Well, it IS Wednesday, so that means market day. Jasmine, Maggie, Juanita and I are headed downtown when we get pulled over for running through an intersection where the lights were out, and almost broadsiding another vehicle. The cop in the intersection points to his eyes and then to Juanita—they often use sign language here. Another street cop on my side motioned for us to pull over. Juanita told us no worries; she can talk her way out of this.

She rolled down the window and started talking to him in Spanish. He finally told her in English to take it easy and relax. They conversed some more, and I heard him repeat *"no problem, no problem"* a few times. He had the ticket in his hand; it was already written up before she opened the window, AND he let her go. Can you believe it? We were all impressed and never asked her exactly what she said to him. All I know is I thought I got away with a lot, but she's better than me. I can learn some tricks from this woman.

I had to remind the girls that it was my fault that she blew through the intersection. You see, I had asked where Dr. Ruiz's office was located (remember the piercing surgeon?), and that caused her to turn her head to point at his street, and take her eyes off the road.

The weather is back, it's about 75 and sunny and we had a fine time at the market, finding treasure after treasure. Of course, there are no dressing rooms, so we were in the isle, trying on clothes. The girls pulled a snug-fitting, funky dress over my head, and convinced me I could not leave without it— the price was right at 45 pesos or around $3. That's how it was that I ended up with a red and black party dress for carnival. Now all I need is a black boa that I will get tomorrow at the fabric store. I have to admit the dress looks much better when I put it on without all my other clothes underneath. After today, we added a number of outfits for the carnival festivities this weekend.

The bras at the market are incredible, table after table of them. They actually could pass for bikini tops. The only way to see if they fit is to put them on over your clothes. A Mexican guy walking by thought this was quite funny and actually picked out a bra for Juanita to try.

We ended the day sitting on the upstairs deck wrapped in blankets and watching the sun sink below the horizon with a Gold Margarita in hand. Later, I wanted a hot shower to relax my thighs, but the showerhead was weird—almost like it was possessed—sputtering, spitting, shooting up off the ceiling and generally pulsating water enough to completely soak the bathroom. Interesting enough, we had just finished a conversation on the deck about the history of spirits in this casa and in Mexico. Apparently, the lady of the original house actually died here. Poltergeists? Coincidence? All of this was running through my head as I struggled with the showerhead. I did manage to get some hot water on the sore legs. Maybe enough so I can walk tomorrow.

Chapter 24 – The Hamburger Sculpture

My legs are okay, a bit sore but manageable. It's a good thing, as Antonio has decided that we have to train for a 2.5k race this Sunday at carnival. So yesterday was an all-leg workout. Aye yi, yi!

The opening of carnival last night was exciting. People were out, the music was loud, and the energy level was high. It began with an epiphany. The city lights went out, and a march through town was lead by torches held by police officers leading an arrested politician through the streets to the town square, where a mock trial was held, the politician was convicted of a crime, and burned.

This event marked the official opening of carnival. Or at least that's the story. We were at the fountain watching Juanita seriously schmooze some police officers and managed to miss the whole thing! It was scheduled to start at 6, but actually happened about 8—hey, it's Mexico and they do everything on their time, not necessarily by the clock.

Today boot camp was a light workout followed by a run the same length as the race on Sunday—about 1-1/2 miles. Okay, so I'm still NOT a runner. But I can run/walk with the best of them. Even though I was slower than Juanita and Maggie, I did finish. And that's what it's all about, si? I'll do fine on Sunday and even get some photographs along the route.

The sun was high and it got warm really quickly. After the workout, we were back on deck for much needed rest and relaxation. I had my second Spanish lesson and I'm even more confused than the first time around. I guess homework would help. I thought I would be able to learn this subliminally, but it's not working. So before Tuesday I will be listing 30 adjectives in English, and the masculine/feminine and singular/plural in Spanish. With a Spanish dictionary I can do this, and hopefully memorize some of the words in the meantime. Putting them together in sentence form is another story . . .

For fun this afternoon I suggested we work with the hamburger again. I saw it sitting in the refrigerator, all seven pounds of it, and wondered where this much weight had been on my body. I needed visuals! So I recruited Maggie and Juanita with an idea of putting it back on my body in places that store fat, and then photographing the result. My boobs, stomach, legs and chin seemed the most likely places.

I went to the casita, got into a bathrobe and headed through the patio area and up the stairs to the private top deck. The girls followed with the seven pounds of ground beef on a platter. Of course, we ran into Antonio working in the garden. He smiled while shaking his head, mumbling something in Spanish, but all I understood was *"Americans."* He obviously had no clue what we were up to and was much too polite to ask. I can only imagine what he was thinking! We did show him the images on the computer later, and he cracked up, still shaking his head!

The hardest part was getting the meat to stick to my skin. We found out early on that laughing was not an option for me. Every time I even so much as moved, the hamburger slid off my body. As difficult as it was, I only giggled a few times. The burger was freezing on my skin, plus it had a gross smell. My collaborators worked quickly at sculpting the meat onto my body. After the photographs were made, I helped Maggie take it off my skin, and ran to the shower to get the grease and smell off me. It's amazing to see that much meat on my body. It doesn't sound like a lot, but try putting it on your body. Weigh-in is on Monday and hopefully now it's even more than the seven pounds documented as of last week. If so, what can I try for a visual next week—sugar, butter, lard?

Chapter 25 - Schmooze Party

Tonight, Maggie and I went to a new restaurant in San Carlos. La Conquista is an elegant restaurant/bar across the street from the Sea of Cortez, serving steak and seafood to the American tourists en mass. We were pleased to see a few local Mexicans there as well. I had seared tuna on a bed of spinach and Maggie had grilled red snapper served with two sauces. We both had a drink, and then another. And for dessert, we each had a gin martini—a bit indulgent tonight. But, the good news? A delicious gourmet meal with three drinks was $22 each, including tip. What a bargain! PLUS, I managed to stay within my diet, while Maggie, in her normal style, cheated.

We decided to go to the party we heard about at the nail salon today; a Who's-Who-in-Guaymas Event—even the governor was going to be there. Apparently he's in town for carnival. A schmoozing party! The party was scheduled to kick off at 10 p.m., but by Mexico time that means more like 11:30. Since it was a costume event, we went home to change our clothes.

Juanita (who had decided to stay home tonight, no matter what was going on!) met us at the gate, so we had to tell her about our dining experience. One conversation lead to another and, before we knew it, an hour had passed. By this time who felt like getting dressed up? Not ME! So, we bagged the party. Neither of us felt like going out again, even though Juanita was beginning to think schmoozing with the governor could be a good thing. That's okay; we'll be fresh for the activities at tomorrow's parade. Who needs a schmooze party anyhow? Juanita can always get up later and go in her bathrobe, and tell us all about it mañana!

Chapter 26 – Carnival Snit

A day off from boot camp – we're not complaining. So, we took it easy around the pool. Luce went in for a new do at the vet clinic—did I mention he does all things dog? And probably all things cat too, for that matter. Juanita is staying home tonight, AGAIN, to get much-needed rest before the big race tomorrow. How old are you really, Juanita?

Around 6 p.m. Maggie and I got dressed up, put on our masks and headed into town for the parade, food and drink. Not necessarily in that order. We don't know the back roads like Juanita, so it wasn't long before we found ourselves in a horrific traffic jam on Serdan. Might as well enjoy it, so we got our cameras out and starting taking pictures while we eased our way closer to town. Interestingly, people in Mexico are very patience and polite. No road rage, horn-blowing or flipping drivers off. Life is much slower here. As we're sitting in traffic a señor poked his head in VeVe's window and said to me, *"How do you like life in Mexico?"* Muy bien, Señor.

We finally made it to Calle 14 and found a parking spot. The festivities were well underway, but the town centre was around Calle 20, so we were in for a hike. The streets were packed with people, and confetti was everywhere. It was then we realized we had missed the parade, AGAIN. Can you believe it? Missed it by about 20 minutes. So we headed in the general direction of the square so Maggie could get some street food. She won't shut up about it, seems she is starving. First things first, though. . . We found an outdoor bar and she ordered a margarita. And what a margarita it was! A 20-oz. cup, and half of it was tequila! Now that's what I call a drink – and for only $4.50! I ordered my usual vodka tonic and it was the same. Huge!

Carne asada was everywhere, but my chicken or fish (diet food this week) was not to be had in the square. This is where Maggie and I had our first snit—one of many. I wanted to go to Poncho Villa for the chicken fajitas because I am sticking to the plan, but she wanted to eat like right now, in front of my face. I insisted that was totally inconsiderate and rude! Finally, Maggie relented and ordered her beef to go, and we headed over to Poncho Villa (drinks in hand) so that I could get chicken—without the chips, rice and beans.

The restaurant was behind the street barricades so we had to walk all the way to Calle 35 to get around and then double back. Whew! By this time we are both starved and thirsty. The 20-oz. drinks were long gone and we were ready for another.

Poncho Villa was standing-room-only, like the entire town. But, we found a barstool and bellied-up to the bar for a menu and drink. The food was delicious and we didn't even get kicked out when Maggie proceeded to eat her street food. We had an adorable waiter that I thought to be about 35, but Maggie had the nerve to ask him in Spanish, how old he was. Forty-five!

After food and drinks we were ready to head home. But we had about 12 blocks to walk first. There were people partying up and down the streets, and the band was just getting started. No dancing in the streets for us tonight—we have a race to run tomorrow, or so I'm told. Who's idea was that? Wouldn't dancing be more fun?

Chapter 27 – Race Day, Holy Shit

Here it is Sunday morning – race day. Why didn't someone remind me that I am not, have not, and will not ever be a runner?

It is a gorgeous day for a carnival race—bright and sunny, with a nice breeze as Team Miramar heads downtown to meet coach Antonio at 11 a.m.—two hours prior to start. Isn't 1 p.m. a bit late for starting a race, at least by U.S. standards? I admit I have entered a few races in North America—the ones where it is totally acceptable to walk/run the entire event, or even just walk, for that matter. There are always people slower than me. If it's a nice day and a T-shirt is involved, I will pay my entry fee and do the course. No pressure, right?

I remember my first "race" back in the '80s. It was New Year's Day in San Diego and my boyfriend at the time suggested we enter a 10k. Not only would we get a free T-shirt marking our participation, at the finish line there would be a beer truck offering all the free beer we could drink. Now that's an incentive! So okay, this was before the entire country went into a health rage outlawing too much fun for exercising. Anyhow, the beer and T-shirt rewards far outweighed the running, so I signed up. It was a fun time and I did not—I repeat, did not—come in last, nor did anyone notice me in the mass of people for that matter. So, that's just a bit of my "running" history. Back to Guaymas and the Sunday afternoon carnival race.

My first clue should have been at sign-up. There were only two categories for women: under 30 and over 30. The men's categories were much more defined in decades. We signed in, paid our entry fee, got a T-shirt (before the run?) and waited for Antonio to arrive. I had decided to bring Zippy along for company because I knew both Juanita and Maggie were faster than me—they have been running for years. Zippy and I could just meander along the course, get some exercise and have some fun.

Antonio arrived and gave me my second clue. Instead of being a 2.5k course, which we had trained for during the last couple of days, it was indeed a 4k race. No exceptions, no alternate starting or ending spots. So instead of 1.2 miles, it was 2.5. In this heat? Yikes!

We did some stretches and trotted to the end of the block and back a couple times. I was trying to look like I knew what I was doing, but why are we running before we have to? Warm-ups? What's that??? Man, was it getting hot; in fact, I'm sweating already and it's 30 minutes before starting time. I look around and there are a handful of men and women in running attire. Where are all the participants? The ones here are extremely serious looking, not to mention BUFF!

I realize Antonio is not in his running clothes and ask why. He tells me that he is not running the race, that the men here run every day, training all year for this race. Wow, now this is serious. I then ask if anyone here is in a walk/run status, and he shakes his head, no. I look around and see the few women participants and realize they all appear to be in their early twenties with legs of steel. I feel myself starting to hyperventilate. Zippy is panting, I'm a wreck, and it's 10 minutes to start. What to do?

Bow out – that's the answer! I simply won't do it. I'm a weenie and I'm so okay with that. This is far too competitive for me, and did I mention serious? About 50 racers jockey for position at the starting line. Juanita and Maggie take their places in the back without me. By this time the sun is high in the sky and it's very hot. I'm feeling grateful that I'm on the sidelines with my camera, Zippy and Antonio; the cheering section feels right. I still have my number pinned on—maybe I could run a kilometer, turn around and head back? Now that would be totally cheating with an unrealistic time, right? Bad karma, but I admit the thought did enter my mind. . . Nah, I'm going to do what I do much better than running - take pictures!

We follow the racers about a mile down the boulevard. I'm hot, Zippy's really hot, but the view of the bay is spectacular. We walk until we see the first guy on his way back to the finish line. He must have been all of 20 years old and very fast. As the racers trickle in, we cheer them on as they pass us. Finally, we see Juanita, and not far behind, Maggie, heading for home stretch with an ambulance trailing close behind. Did they think Team Miramar was going to collapse on the spot? Not a chance.

Team Miramar (lacking one) crossed the finish line looking good! Juanita and Maggie were on an endorphin high, sweating, and so glad to be finished! It was at this point that Zippy collapsed at my feet. She was way too hot. Coach Antonio brought water to pour over her to cool her body temperature down. She was not only soaking up the water, but also all the attention she was getting

In the meantime, the winners were being announced. The male winners were by age categories and there were many.

When it got to the female winners, there were only the two divisions. Now is that discrimination or what? Not really, because there were only about 10 women total! Running is not a big sport for the women of Mexico. But the ones who do run are young, gorgeous and very FIT.

When they announced in Spanish the third-place winner in the over-30, I hear Maggie say, "*That's me,*" and off to the podium she went with a big smile, followed by Juanita in second place - GO TEAM! Both of them were glowing. What an exciting finish. Never mind that there were only four racers in this category – the fourth being yours truly.

Team Miramar raced and placed, and was rewarded 300 pesos each, which was donated back to the race fund for next year. Antonio was proud of his girls. It was now time for a beer, but there was no beer truck at this finish line. Basking in our success as a team, we headed off to the bar for food and drinks—much deserved food and drinks. Team Miramar treated coach and his family to lunch while Zippy slept in the backyard of the restaurant. Totally spent. Antonio announced that boot camp was canceled for tomorrow.

Wow, what a day! And the best part? My last-minute decision to be a photographer instead of a runner! And, I have pictures to prove it. This was definitely not the race for a

Silly Woman!

Chapter 28 – Froggies

It's a beautiful Monday morning and a day off from boot camp—what a good way to start the week. We're off to Guaymas early so that we can weigh in before breakfast, although my appetite is next to none. Maggie's along so she can sign up, get a diet plan, the laser zap and acupressure. I am pleased to report that I have lost another kilo, or 2.2 pounds. If I keep this up I will definitely be skinny when I leave Mexico in April.

My fourth-week diet plan includes ham and eggs, papaya, carne asada, chicken, salad, cottage cheese, and toast. And, the usual tequila, vodka, rum and whiskey are okay. Not bad, huh? And the food here is so good. I thought the chickens seemed so small and then realized it's because they are not full of growth hormones and preservatives. Duhhh!

The temperature has been hotter the last several days but cools off considerably when the sun sets. A day by the pool with a good book and iced *agua mineral* sounds great. Casa Miramar is going to be hopping later this week, with John and Anne arriving from Vashon/France, Cathy from Oregon and Maggie moving to San Carlos to free up the guest room. We are talking about having our "coming-out" party next week and that requires some planning—invitations, finding a DJ, catering, etc. It is all about people, dancing, food and drink, right?

Speaking of dancing. . . Jasmine called and invited the three of us over for dinner. She also signed up at the diet center today and suggested that we have grilled pollo, asparagus and salad – all on our diet plan. A bottle of rum with some lime and Coca Light is in order – Cuba Libres at Jasmine and Dave's new palapa on the roof—a celebration of the weight loss and their new addition. We had one, then another, and maybe a third. As the sun set on the horizon, the sky was alive with blue, pink, red and gold colors. Someone suggested that it was time to eat, finally. These drinks have gone to my head and apparently everyone else's, too.

We scarfed down the food—Dave did a wonderful job of grilling the chicken. Mexican music was playing in the background as more drinks were poured and we were up and moving about in a gang dance. Mexican music has a way of bringing people to their feet! I was trying to take pictures but people were moving so fast and the point-and-shoot had a delay; I got a lot of blurred images. Oh well, they are indicative of the evening. Dave just hung out and mixed drinks with this stunned look on his face. I decided it was time to go to Froggies, on foot. Dave bowed out, smiling and shaking his head as Maggie, Juanita, Jasmine and I headed to the bar.

Froggies was very quiet—is it Monday or what? We tried hard to liven it up but the gringos were having none of it. Especially when Juanita included herself in a serious pool game. She was just trying to show the guy how to hold his stick. He actually walked out of the bar. Jeeez, no sense of humor! Gringos can be so uptight. Nevertheless, we had a couple more drinks—now that's what we needed—along with a few laughs, and then headed back. I should mention that Maggie was the DD so she had very little to drink. It is really a big job watching everyone else get toasted when you're straight—not that I've ever done it. We walked back to Jasmine's casa in San Carlos and said our Mexican goodbyes, which means hugging, kissing and saying gracias more than once.

The next part I am writing is totally from hearsay. I vaguely remember the details, but Maggie shared them later with both Juanita and me. We laughed so hard our stomachs are sore. So I know it's really hard to believe. . . Rumor has it that Silly Woman can get a bit obnoxious after consuming a few beverages. Apparently, we were at a stoplight on the way home and I made eye contact with a gentleman on Maggie's side of the car. I asked her to roll the window down and she said no—not a good thing to say to Silly Woman when she's been drinking. We bantered back and forth, ending with me saying, *"Roll the fucking window down!"* At that, she rolled the window down. In my sweetest voice I say, *"Hola,"* and the guy replies, *"Hola."* And then my mind went blank. Apparently, that's all the Spanish I could remember at the moment. Maggie waited a few seconds and then rolled the window back up. Of course, this really pissed me off. I wanted to talk to him, but she told me I already had. We continued arguing back and forth in yet another snit, until finally the light changed and we were out of there. Forgotten in a flash, apparently.

I don't know, it sounds a little exaggerated to me. Some of this could be a figment of Maggie's imagination. Especially since Juanita doesn't remember either. It doesn't really ring true that Silly Woman was obnoxious. ME?

Chapter 29 – The Hangover from Hell

Did we really drink that much last night? I'm feeling spacier than normal this morning, maybe because I got up at 4? We are back to the grind this morning with boot camp. Antonio was late, so Maggie, Juanita and I did our warm-up and went for a run without coach. After some work with weights, we had another day by the pool, just relaxing and hanging out. Or at least some of us did. Juanita and Maggie were busy getting Casa Miramar ready for the guests coming in.

I had just gotten out of the shower when Juanita poked her head in for a visit. What she saw was me with a towel around my head and a matching one around my body. Now that was a picture, or so she thought. Nothing is sacred here because someone always has a camera. Not only that, but she yelled for Maggie to come over, and they both decided some plastic fruit pieces on top of my hair towel would be perfect. Okay, whatever—as long as the towel doesn't drop off, I'm game. I'm not entirely sure what I'm supposed to look like in these images. But, the process of sticking bananas and tomatoes on top of my head seemed very funny at the time. And every time I giggled, something fell off and had to be rearranged.

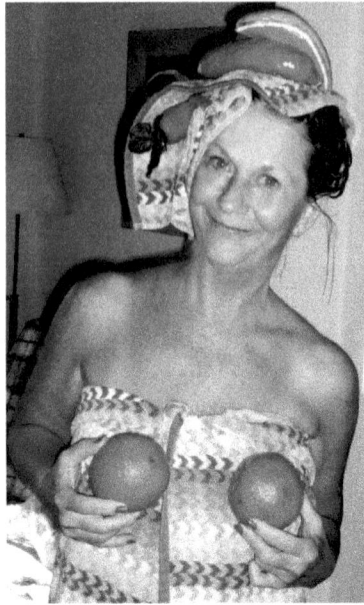

Later in the afternoon we went to San Carlos. Maggie was moving into Gretchen's beachfront home for a few days, while Anne and John visit. They are arriving on the bus from Tucson tonight. We debated on meeting them in full costume; after all, it IS Fat Tuesday. But, since we had our party last night, we blew off that idea.

Juanita and I returned to Guaymas for my 5 p.m. appointment with Dr. Sergio Ruiz (remember the piercing surgeon?). I am having my ears re-pierced today, but the real reason I made another appointment was to photograph the doc in his sunglasses and red sports car.

We arrive in his office and there he is. No flashy arrival

like before. How disappointing, and where is that red sports car? Oh well, he proceeded to pierce my ears—two holes on each, and once again I am stunned that he had finished the job in record time without causing me any pain. They look great. He asked about my bellybutton and if I liked it. He had another look to be sure it was healing okay, and said it looked beautiful. I think Italians use that word a lot.

Okay, so I have to ask him about the car. He said he left it home today, and home, wouldn't you know it, is in Miramar a stone's throw from our house. I told him that my real plan, or most of it, was to photograph him for my friends. He really liked that idea and said he would bring his car to the office whenever I wanted to come back for the photo op. He even agreed to the suit jacket and dark glasses! In the meantime, I got him to pose for a headshot in the waiting room. We left with a promise to return and get the other shot sometime this week. Jasmine told me last night that I should go for it (him)?

On the way home, I took a definite nose-dive. I could still feel the Cuba Libres from last night and needed to crash. Hopefully, I will wake up more coherent than I've been all day. Did I mention that I got up this morning at 4 because I couldn't sleep? Well, now I can and it's only 6 p.m. I have to get my rest because tomorrow is Wednesday, and you know what that means—market day! Life is good for a Silly Woman, even with a hangover.

Chapter 30 – Running the Caracoles, Seriously?

It's the weekend! Not that the day really matters here in Guaymas. One day runs into the next without me even knowing, except for Wednesdays—market day— and Saturday/Sunday because there is no boot camp.

Last night Maggie, Juanita and I took John and Anne to La Conquista, the awesome new restaurant in San Carlos. I had a rib-eye steak (on the diet) that was to die for. Probably on the list of the best 10 steaks I've ever had, with ensalada and asparagus, not to mention two martinis. We got home early in preparation for today's run up the Caracols—a large, gated, hill community in San Carlos, full of gringos. It reminds me of the Petragal in Cabo.

In some ways it is really great not understanding the conversation going on around me. I vaguely heard that we were "running" up the Caracols today for our workout and didn't understand exactly what that meant. It's a good thing because, had I known, I would have backed out and simply run on the beach. Oh well. Here's how it went.

We picked up Maggie in San Carlos around 8 a.m. and headed to the Caracols. Maggie was talking non-stop in a rapid flow of unconsciousness. If only I could have recorded this. . .

one comment led to another, and yet another totally unrelated topic. No one said anything in the van—who had time to do anything but listen? Maggie finally admitted to having three cups of Nescafé instant coffee. OMG, now it makes sense. Who drinks instant coffee anymore? If her behavior is any indication, the caffeine content has to be off the chart. Juanita made a racquetball analogy that seemed to fit. Maggie went to Alamos with Jasmine and Dave after our workout. I wonder if she ran out of steam or is talking their ear off in the car?

We arrived at the Caracols and I couldn't believe we were actually going to run up that hill. Not this girl. You see, Juanita is actually training for a stair race in Seattle in mid-March – something like 1,600 stairs. Yikes! And she's competing with her buddy, Bruce. So for her, this is serious business.

The streets of the Caracols are cobblestone and steep, so I tell Antonio after warm-up that I will be walking the route. Not a problem. They set off jogging and so did I for a short distance. But I'm concerned about tripping and falling, not to mention breathing, so I quickly slow down to a walking pace. Obviously I fall behind as the street winds up the hill and comes to a Y, and then another, and still another. Okay, so they are long gone and I have to make a decision on which way to turn at each stop—a 50-50 chance, right? Well, you guessed it; I picked the wrong one on at least one occasion.

My understanding was that we would run up the hill and then come down on the other side. Sounds easy enough. I love the downhill part. So I head downhill, ending up at the beach. But, where is the marina? I see two guys in a car and wave them over to ask about the marina. They point to a palm tree at the very top of the hill (the one I just came down) and tell me I have to go there, turn right up another hill in order to get to the other side. I say that I don't want to do any more hills; can't I get there from here? Only if you want to swim, was their reply. And I couldn't bear to ask for a ride. What would the team think if they saw me in a car?

GAWD! So now I have to climb back up the damn hill for who knows how far? Where are they? Maybe they will come looking for me in the car—fat chance. Suck it up, get it over with, and smile in the process, is what I told myself. So I did. This area looks very European, and the exercise is good for me and will show at weigh in on Monday. Amazing how much it helps just to change my perspective of the task at hand.

Back up the hill I go and at the top I meet up with Team

Miramar on their way down. Somewhere along the line I had taken more than one wrong turn. Oh well, we're together now and I don't mind the running downhill. At least I'm not winded and I can finish with the team if I don't trip on the cobblestones in the process.

Back to Casa Miramar for my second Spanish lesson for the week. We are learning phrases in the present tense now. I need to study, but when do I have time? There is so much fun to be had and no time left. I admitted to Francisco that my plan was to wake up some morning and speak Spanish fluently. He just smiled and shook his head.

Cathy comes tomorrow, so that means another week of fun in the sun. She mentioned getting her nose pierced. Oh boy, another reason to go back to see Dr. Ruiz and get that photograph. And, who knows what's in store for boot camp next week?

Chapter 31 – Musical Beds

Cathy arrived at the Guaymas airport at 4:15 Saturday afternoon—one flight a day and it's a prop plane. We went to the casita for a welcome drink, and then out to dinner with the crew of John, Anne and Juanita. Dinner was in San Carlos at an outdoor restaurant, which would have been great at sunset, but by this time it was already dark. So the view of the sea was just a black void. Juanita and I ordered fish tacos with the intention of just eating the stuff inside without the tortillas. Dinner came and, much to our surprise, the fish was deep-fried. Oh no, we can't eat that. Juanita proceeded to tell the waiter that we needed grilled fish. So they made our special-request tacos, and they were scrumptious!

Rajulio and his wife arrived Saturday afternoon on their way to Vashon, so they are sleeping on the roof with an air mattress. Anne and John have the guest bedroom, and I'm in the casita with the dogs. Maggie is off to Alamos with Jasmine and Dave for a couple days. So Cathy has Gretchen's beautiful seaside house to herself tonight until Maggie returns tomorrow. It is definitely the swinging doors here at Casa Miramar. Neighborhood people were partying in the streets last night like they often do on weekends. However, Juanita must have slept through everything because there was no mention of her out dancing after midnight.

Cathy and I went to the Humane Society chili cook-off Sunday afternoon in San Carlos. Each booth had a different variety of chili, from vegetarian, beans and beef, no beans, green chili with pork, and even reindeer chili. You name it and it was probably there. I could only sample the beanless type. With our donations, we ended up with about 50 tickets to buy chili, ice cream (I don't think so), beer (another no-no) and yummy looking pastries (not). There was not much that fit into my diet here. So in the end we had about 40 tickets left and decide to donate them to the guitar player on stage. When we offered him our tickets, he smiled and asked us if he could buy beer with them. We told him to knock himself out; he could get whatever he wanted on us!

Back to the casita, into the bathing suits and out to the recliners by the pool with a good book. We read, chat, read, sleep, read and relax. Antonio told me that his favorite tequila was Sauza so when I saw it at the mercado, I got a bottle and put it in the freezer. Well, after all that reading, sleeping, chatting and relaxing it was time for a sip. I poured ice cold sippin' tequila into two shot glasses and topped them off with a lime slice. It was so delicious that we had another. About this time Maggie called from San Carlos. The Alamos crew was back and she was locked out of Gretchen's house. So much for sippin' more now—I have to go pick her up.

We had decided to go to La Playa for a drink at sunset that is only a few blocks from Casa Miramar. La Playa is the oldest colonial hotel in Guaymas, built in the 1930s. Many movies have been filmed there, including Catch-22 and The Mask of Zorro. The setting is gorgeous, overlooking the ocean and mountains.

We piled into Juanita's van—everyone except Juanita, who has elected to stay home and rest. We will miss her, but understand her need to be away from all of us for a little while. It has been non-stop all weekend. The waiter at La Playa brought our drinks out to the lawn by the sea—a nice hike from the bar. He has worked here 40-plus years and knows how to make his customers happy.

It's now dinnertime, so we head to another outdoor restaurant, this one in Guaymas. We have a delicious meal, and then I take Cathy and Maggie back to San Carlos and head home. I know it sounds like we eat, drink and drive a lot. Well, that's what weekends are for, right?

Tomorrow we're back to the usual Guaymas grind: boot

camp in the morning, weigh-in with the diet doctor, and then out to lunch to celebrate. Life is good for a Silly Woman in Mexico!

Chapter 32 – Hoes R Us

When I got home last night, I discovered the tequila mouse had been by for a visit. My laundry room door that leads to the big house was open, but the dogs were sound asleep. The bottle of tequila that had been about one-quarter full was sitting on the counter, completely empty. A tequila mouse in the house? The dogs? I don't think so. Or, JUANITA! So much for being home alone. . . and she thought I wouldn't notice!

Boot camp is back in full swing this morning. Antonio made us individual torture bands for our leg stretches. After some warm-up stretches, we did a run on the beach, and I AM getting better. I actually ran more than I walked today and didn't quite complain as much. Back to the casa for more calisthenics, ending with our favorite abdominal crunches!

Maggie just got back from Alamos where she cheated on the diet, as USUAL. I have been the diet Nazi with her lately, but it really doesn't do any good. She interprets the list of food in her own way. In fact, she tried to recruit Jasmine to do the same on their weekend trip, telling her that what they did in Alamos was between them. Sorry, Maggie. Jasmine told all—you're such a bad influence, girl.

The woman eats more than anyone I know, has a very high

metabolism and is already thin. John mentioned this morning that since she cheats so much, it might get ugly at weigh-in if she actually loses more than Juanita and I. The scales will soon tell the story.

Another 1.5 kilos for me, and .5 for Juanita! Yes! But Maggie came in at 2 kilos. I have to admit she was humble about her weight loss. She did win, but she blamed it on lots of things, including the fact that she had just eliminated prior to weigh-in—Whatever! I was happy with my results. Juanita has reached a plateau, but still it's a loss and she's doing great. It's her seventh week, my fifth and Maggie's second (bitch). And that's about as ugly as it got. All in all, we were all extremely happy campers.

When Juanita got her acupressure zap, I heard her say, *"Una mas."* What a good idea! Of course, I started my session with *"Una mas"* as well, meaning one more, please. We each got two zaps instead of the usual one per week. The second jolt went through my jaw, across my chest and out my opposite thumb. Wow! Now that was a ZAP.

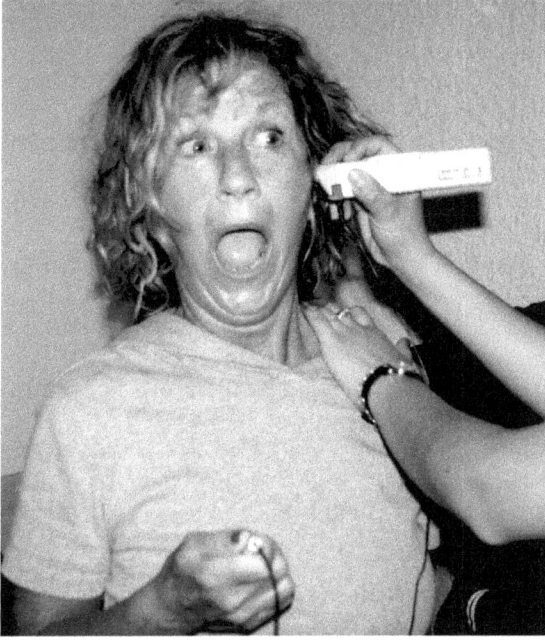

My diet for this week includes: cereal with light milk and fresh-squeezed OJ for breakfast, yogurt or a piece of fruit for a snack, carne asada, pollo or pescado with vegetables and salad for lunch and dinner. Not a bad diet, actually extremely filling. The challenge is to make something creative out of the choices.

To celebrate the fruits of our labor (so to speak), John and Anne suggested we go to Empalme for lunch. Cathy, Juanita, John, Anne, Maggie and I piled into the van. The orders varied, but our table was soon decorated with grilled white fish, vegetables, ensalada, guacamole, piña coladas, lemonada con gas, shrimp wrapped in bacon and garlic pescado

– guess what the diet queens ate? It wasn't the guacamole!

We decided John needed to drive us, so in the van headed back to Guaymas the rest of us were discussing the merits of being in a foreign country, and changing our work identities. Wouldn't it be fun to "pretend" to be something we're not? And what would that be? Maggie said she would like to be a forensic anthropologist (whatever that means); Juanita, a psychotherapist; and me? Well those things were much too scientific for me. I like simple. I said I wanted to be a high-priced hoe, which caused a round of giggles. First I had to define a "hoe" to Juanita, with everyone's help!

John could not contain himself so he suggested it was a great idea for a new line of business and could possibly be a moneymaker if we marketed ourselves as the "Elder Hoes," or the "Geri-Hoes." And then someone else came up with the byline "Hoes R Us." We thought this was hysterical. We were laughing so hard our sides were aching by the time we got back to Guaymas. Are we funny or WHAT? John had to be a wee bit overwhelmed in the company of five silly women and no male compadres. I'm sure he got a real insight into what women talk about when they get together. Or at least he thinks he did.

After all this joking around it was time for a nap by the

pool. Having so much fun can be exhausting! Cathy and I finished off the evening by visiting Jasmine (who lost over 2 kilos on her first week) and Dave for a drink and back to Gretchen's for a shot of Absolut Pear. Tasty enough to be addictive!

Tomorrow, things change at Casa Miramar as some people leave and others rotate in. I have to say there is never a dull moment here in Guaymas.

Chapter 33 – The Hair Salon

The crowd left for the bus station at 6 a.m. Rajulio has his Green Card and will cross into the United States without a problem. However, his wife is being escorted through the mountains in an attempt to cross over with five others. She is only 21 and does not speak English. The coyote will charge $3,500 once she reaches the U.S. If everything goes as planned, Rajulio will meet up with her in Los Angeles and they will continue their trek to the Pacific Northwest.

John and Anne will return to Vashon Island, where it is still rainy and cold—sorry guys. John is a residential architect with projects to finish, and Anne will be leaving for her home in Normandy on March 18. She spends nine months out of the year in France, and has applied for residency. Zippy has been invited to visit Normandy, where dogs go everywhere with their people, even restaurants. There is an Air France direct flight to Paris from Seattle—9-1/2 hours instead of the 22 hours required to go back east and over. I guess that means we'll be getting our tickets real soon for the fall.

Maggie left for Copper Canyon and a bus/train trip for a few days. Cathy is moving from Gretchen's house in San Carlos to Casa Miramar for the rest of her stay in Mexico. And, everything else is as it should be in Guaymas.

We had a reprieve from boot camp since Antonio's daughter was performing in a dance recital this morning. Juanita and I went to the school and watched the kids dance on stage in their brightly colored costumes. Dance is an integral part of Mexican culture and the kids learn at a very young age. Wish I could move my shoulders like that!

Both of us decided we needed a hairdresser, so on the way home we found a salon that was recommended by a friend. We had quite a time finding this salon. We actually stopped to ask three different people, finally using the cell phone to call and ask directions. This was our first clue that this might be a bad idea. I've learned that when you force things, they sometimes get ugly. Juanita made an appointment for later today and mine is tomorrow.

We returned to the casa and I picked up VeVe and headed over to San Carlos to pick up Cathy and get her things moved to Guaymas. On the way home we shopped for the nose jewelry we needed for our visit to the piercing surgeon. The rest of the afternoon was spent lounging by the pool while Juanita went for her hair appointment. She came home with a story. . .

Apparently, when she arrived at the salon, the stylist

refused to talk to her—not a good thing when you're trying to tell her what you want in a color and cut. Juanita tried to engage her in conversation; her Spanish is quite good and she communicates very well, but she could not understand the stylist, who was speaking very fast slang Spanish to everyone around her and totally ignoring Juanita. Juanita referred to her as the "shithead bitch," among other things.

Once the foil was in her hair, Juanita was left alone for it to process. As she is sitting there, she is getting madder and madder thinking how dare she stereotype me as a rich American from San Carlos. How dare she ignore me when I'm a paying customer. How can I get her attention? And then she got an idea . . .

Juanita simply rolled off the chair onto the floor in a fake fainting, foiled head and all. And it worked! Everyone in the shop came running over to this woman lying in a heap on the floor. They wanted to know if she was okay, did she need water, did she need a doctor, what could they do to help. All the while Juanita is thinking: Now this is more like it. She finally got the attention she deserved. And she is crying; real tears are rolling down her cheeks. I presume this crying act was an attempt to keep the giggles under control. Juanita, have you ever thought about Hollywood?

The rest of her experience was much better. Keep in mind this salon did not have running water, so they used buckets of water to pour over her head to get the chemicals out. Yikes! But they did it cheerfully, and never again ignored her. Her hair color/cut is okay, although she wanted something a little more extravagant. She was just glad she still had hair when she got out of there. And you think I'm keeping my appointment tomorrow? NOT!

We finished off the day with dinner at Poncho Villa, chicken fajitas, AGAIN. But they are soooo good and on the diet. We were celebrating the fainting performance. Juanita is not normally a drama queen (or is she?), but today? Well, I get it. Just don't fuck with Juanita.

Chapter 34 - The Photo Op

More running and exercise. It feels good and I am actually getting better at this. I still don't love it, but that's okay. Antonio is teaching me how to breathe and pace myself and it really makes a difference. I still want to know what it feels like when the endorphins kick in. How far do I have to run for that to happen?

It's Wednesday and we're taking Cathy to market—the Wednesday market in Guaymas, to shop for things we don't need. But it's about fun and not need, right? Juanita found a black lace top that fits me like a corset. I squeezed into it over all my clothes—talk about tight, but it does suck everything in.

Will I ever wear all these les trés jours? It's so much about the search, and Juanita is a master at finding things. Like the French dress—with lots of blue and red flowers and pink trim—that looks more like a slip than a dress. I had to have it. And the real kicker? A short dress that shows lots of cleavage! It pushes me up, and almost over and out. In Mexico it is very appropriate. But in Homer, Alaska, where sweats are the style, I dunno.

How many party dresses have I found at the market?

Maybe four? And that doesn't include the ones in Vashon from Granny's Attic that I have stored. I'll need to buy a van to get all these things back to Alaska. But then maybe I don't want to take them back to Alaska. Decisions to think about later! But for now, buy, buy, buy. Where else can you have so much fun for under $20? By the time our shopping frenzy is over, we have a ton of bags to carry and can't really remember everything we have. It's time for a review over lunch. I have lost my appetite completely so settle for a lemonada con gas for an entrée.

We return to Casa Miramar but have no time for lounging by the pool today because Cathy has an appointment to have her nose violated. Sergio, the piercing surgeon (we are now on a first-name basis), is charming as ever and did a great nose piercing on her. He brought his red sports car and looked ready for the photo op. However when we return to the waiting room area, it was overflowing with patients. Sergio ushers another one into his office, closing the door just as I realize my car keys are on the counter in the exam room. I had asked earlier about a photograph but see now that it will be awhile before he is free. But I do need my keys before we can leave.

In a flash (did he read my mind?), he walks out of the exam room, says something in Spanish to his next patient, hands me my keys and follows us out the door. He's ready for a photo session and his patients are apparently okay with waiting. I take a few shots, Cathy takes a few shots and we say goodbye with the usual cheek-to-cheek kissing, and a promise to come back next week for my nose piercing. What a flirt, but also a good surgeon. His piercings are pain free.

Cathy and I met Juanita at the cinema to see Richard Gere's new movie—okay, so I like Richard Gere. It was totally my idea to go, and the movie turned out to be hard-core violence. I can't even remember the name of it, but I know it was very disturbing. Needless to say, I got a lot of grief for the suggestion.

I have totally fallen in love with Mexico, the people and the culture—their approach to life is very basic and relaxing. Life is simple in Guaymas. What more can I say?

Chapter 35 – Froggies, Again?

Thursday morning is running and calisthenics, the usual. Maybe we need to hold a boot camp week for visitors in Guaymas? I would love to introduce others to this great workout and diet plan. Cathy and I relax by the pool and have another Spanish lesson. I need to study and memorize more, but I have to admit it is starting to make sense and that's a good thing.

Tomorrow night is the festival at Casa Miramar. We are inviting all who want to come. Cathy and I are shopping today and it occurs to us that we need to invite Sergio, the incredible piercer. We stop by his office and he is delighted by the invitation. I told him to bring his wife—he has one, or maybe two! But we run into the language problem. I can't tell him how to get to the casa in a way he understands. I took his card and told him Juanita would call with directions.

Juanita's two sisters (and spouses) are arriving tonight and she has a commitment to a welcoming party for them in San Carlos. No problem, Cathy wants to have a steak at La Conquista anyhow (the place with wonderful steaks and martinis). We arrive at the restaurant and get the full attention of the staff—and we don't even have to fake a fainting. We order our martinis and then our steaks. A couple more drinks and we're out of there. Sated and happy! Life is good.

I realize Cathy has not been to Froggies and that is a requirement in San Carlos. Froggies, the redneck bar, where smoking is the norm and tolerance is the lesson. Politically incorrect, and we love it! We're here to have some fun. We order a couple drinks, Cathy has a Zombie (really?) and me, rum and Coca Light. There are lots of gringos with dogs that I can talk to. We are finishing our drinks and getting ready to leave, when who walks in? Juanita! After her dinner party she was on the way home, saw VeVe in the parking lot, did a U-turn and ended up at the bar with us. Go figure! We're in trouble now.

This calls for a celebration, so I say *"una mas"*—one more, while Juanita tells us about her evening. Of course, the pool table is calling her and she cannot resist. She has a need to tell the players again how to hold their sticks. Plus, Cathy puts her name on the board to play. After a few more pool games we realize that Cathy's name has been totally ignored. Good thing Juanita is here to straighten things out. No way are they going to overlook Cathy. Juanita talks to the players and I see

Cathy racking up the balls with Juanita telling the guys how it is. In the meantime, Silly Woman is singing karaoke to Black Velvet. I barely know that song but am having a great time faking it! All I can remember is una mas—at least five times! Yikes! We stayed much longer than we expected but had a grand time singing GAWD knows what with other people in the bar. We thought we were awesome, maybe we were???? I doubt it, but who really cares?

Cathy and I drove home in VeVe, and Juanita in her car. It's late, we've had a few too many, and we are happy. And tomorrow night is the festival at Casa Miramar. Buenas noches, hasta mañana.

Chapter 36 - Jell-O Shooter Time!

Needless to say, things were a bit slow getting started today. Juanita and Cathy actually have colds, so we decided to have a day of rest from boot camp. It's time for some pampering instead.

On our way to San Carlos, Cathy and I are stopped at a census road survey. They asked me all the usual questions—how much I spend a month, where I am staying, where I am going, and the final one was: What is your age? Without missing a beat, I replied, 39. He wrote it down, smiled and said, *"muchas gracias,"* as Cathy fell off her seat laughing. De nada, sir, as I closed the window and moved on. What?

We took Woody to the vet for his grooming appointment only to find the vet had no water—it had been off for two days, plus he had an emergency surgery on the way. He apologized and said to come back on Monday; the water would be back on. He noticed that Woody had a spot on his nose that was bleeding—no, he did not have it pierced, I know that's what you were thinking. Solomon (first-name basis with the vet, too) told me to put him on the table. He cleaned the scratch and sprayed silver on it. That's right, SILVER. I looked at Cathy. . . weird. Cathy later told me that silver is an excellent antibiotic; she is a M.D., so she should know. All of this and the vet did not charge me a penny. I just love how everyone is so caring and accommodating in Mexico.

We have to get something to eat before our pedicure appointment. Hangovers NEED junk food, so we head to the local Jak Snack—the equivalent of a fast-food place in the States. I order a hamburger, no bun, a salad, no fries, and water. This diet has changed the way I eat, and the way I think about food. We took our Jak Snack to a table outside next to the street, so that Woody could be with us.

A pedicure is one thing here where you can totally zone out. The procedure is completely done by hand, and the feet are filed for at least 20 minutes each. The technician speaks only Spanish so there is no need for idle chitchat. It's easy to meditate, fall asleep sitting up, or just observe all the activities going on in the salon. After a couple hours, we emerged feeling rested, and with funky toes to show for it. I wanted four different colors painted on my toes. That was a challenge to communicate, but she just called a girl over that spoke English and she did the painting.

We returned to the casa, Juanita called Sergio with directions, and we prepared the house and patio for the festival. Juanita had decided this was going to be a dessert party. And what are we suppose to eat, I wondered? We can have Light Jell-O, so why not make some shooters? Lime Jell-O made with hot water and cold rum. Finally, a way to make Jell-O tolerable.

Juanita, Jasmine and I can also have some of the fruit, but we do have to ignore the FIVE cakes from the bakery, along with the cookies. This has to be a test of willpower, but actually we commented on how we have lost all desire to indulge in sweet stuff. Well, most of us, anyhow. Instead, we get our kicks from watching everyone else eat it!

The guests arrive and the shooters were a big hit—they actually took your breath away! Guess I was a little heavy handed with the rum, but they were still delicious. It was a quiet party, which is just what Juanita, Cathy and I had hoped for. Sergio arrived and told us he was running for presidential political office, which equates to the mayor. Now that was interesting.

Antonio arrived with his family, the sisters and spouses; Jasmine and Dave, Connie and John, Kay and Steve, a couple down the street just arrived today from Reno, and some other drop-ins. The girls spent time in Juanita's closet looking at all the treasures from the tienda. It was fun, but we were happy that it ended early. Cathy leaves tomorrow, so it will once again be me, the dogs and Juanita until Maggie returns from the Canyon.

Currently, all is quiet at Casa Miramar, with the exception of Foreigner on the radio singing URGENT. A blast from the '80s.

Chapter 37 - The Soggy Peso

It's Saturday morning and a break from boot camp. Juanita has a full-blown cold and her voice is fading and a bit squeaky. She decided today is her day of much needed rest.

Cathy and I blew off our Spanish lessons for a lunch date at the Soggy Peso restaurant with the men's softball team. Jasmine, Dave and the gang invited us last night and, since Cathy has a plane to catch at 4:50 this afternoon (back to Oregon and the snow), it sounds like a good send-off lunch for her.

The Hangout Bar (next to the restaurant) is located on the other side of the bay in San Carlos—beautiful white sand beaches with dogs running in the surf. It's basically a beach bar with tacos, tostadas, chips and guacamole, margaritas, and cervezas. Not much for a diet girl to eat. It's a good thing my appetite was left with the acupressure doctor.

I ordered my normal lemonada con gas and passed on the food, except for the four chips, broken into small pieces, that I allow myself to have occasionally. By breaking the chips up, it forces me to eat slowly—have you ever dipped tiny pieces of chips into salsa? Well then, you know what I mean. Cathy ordered one last margarita, guacamole and chips, and a crab tostada that looked really good. After lunch, the girls migrated to the bar where a local jeweler had set up silver jewelry, made exclusively by his family. I ended up with a pair of dangling fish earrings that started out being 350 pesos, but I eventually paid 250—less than $20.

Cathy and I returned to Casa Miramar to collect her things, sit in the sun for an hour and have one last cocktail—an ice-cold shot of Absolut Peach. We arrive at the Guaymas airport just in time to say goodbye, had a great time, can't believe the week went so fast, etc. Adios, amiga. See you soon. Back home I have another Absolut Peach with Juanita. I'm swearing off the booze next week. After this week, I NEED a break from drinking! And weigh-in is on Monday. Will I actually gain weight from the liquid indulgence? Yikes!

Chapter 38 – Just Another Weigh-In

I'm feeling a bit nervous that I have put on weight with all the beverages this past week, but I did stick to the food plan. Imagine my surprise when I heard the diet doctor say one more kilo—2.2 pounds! This can become addictive. I feel so lean and light these days. And the appetite is barely there at all. This is by far the best way I have found to eat, feel good, and stay in shape. I don't feel deprived, and that's a good thing. I will definitely miss the fresh vegetables, natural beef, chicken and fish, along with the yummy fruits when I go back to the other side.

For week six the plan is simple: a smoothie consisting of papaya and milk (I also add ice, cinnamon and vanilla) in the morning; a glass of fresh-squeezed OJ or grapefruit juice for a snack; ensalada with beef or chicken for lunch; and another smoothie for dinner. Is that easy or what? I will alternate with ground beef cooked with spices and vinegar in lettuce rolls, sautéed chicken with vegetables, or carne asada with peppers and onions for lunch. This plan forces me to be creative with the few items I do get for the week. Very basic, healthy and delicious!

After weigh-in and grocery shopping, we are back to the

casa to take Woody for his grooming appointment in San Carlos. While he's at the vet, I search for a dentist to clean my teeth. The first office I stopped at was called The American Dental Clinic—and the price was about $55. I decided to keep looking and found a Mexican dentist who quoted me $40—now that's a bargain! My appointment is set for Friday.

The casita is a wonderful space to hang out for the afternoon. I'm almost finished with "Zone of Tolerance," a book written by David Stuart about life in Guaymas in the 1970s. I will share a couple of paragraphs comparing sounds and smells with the U.S. that particularly resonate with my experience here.

"Even restaurants in the two countries sounded as if they had been constructed on two different planets. Mexican restaurants have a sharp, ringing clatter characteristic of hard-tiled surfaces and few curtains, upholstery, or wall hangings to soften the sound. Most Stateside restaurants tend toward the sedate. Hushed, soft lights, carpet, fat chairs. Somber - rather like funeral parlors where food happens to be served."

"And as for smells, the States simply doesn't. Bland.

Deodorized, except for occasional hints of Pine-Sol and gasoline. A nation that has, for some odd reason, given itself the equivalent of an olfactory hysterectomy. In short, I was soon to reenter 'the richest nation on earth,' but one that sometimes came off as intent upon social and sensory deprivation."

Chapter 39 – Forever Wanderlust

The locals told us the hot spell last week was only temporary. Today the sun is out but the temperature is back to normal for this time of year. That means about 80 degrees during the day, dropping down to the 60s after sunset, with a breeze off the ocean.

Boot camp is easier without the heat. I actually ran today without stopping to walk. You could say I am getting the hang of it. Although I don't particularly like the running part, I really love the feeling at the end. I guess that's why I keep doing it. And once the exercise is over, we have the entire day to relax.

We picked up Juanita's two sisters, in San Carlos for lunch. The marina has a good restaurant and, since I've not been there, we decide to check it out. Our table is on the deck overlooking the sailboats in the harbor. The sun is shining and the water is a vibrant turquoise. We order grilled pollo with ensalada – hold the arroz y frijoles, por favor. No beverages today other than agua on the rocks.

Juanita's brother-in-law seems to think I should move to Eastport, Maine, the northernmost part of Maine near Nova Scotia. And why would I want to do that? He is a potter/painter and they own an art gallery there. Apparently, Eastport is an art community with an eclectic group of talented artists, writers, musicians and the like. The Alaska poet laureate, Tom Sexton, spends his winters in Eastport— from Alaska to Maine in the winter? Go figure. But maybe it's not about the weather. . .

I don't know, this tropical weather seems to agree with me more than the ice and snow and I do believe it is colder in Maine than in Homer, Alaska. Eastport looks like a wonderful community and the prices are right – a 6,000-square-foot house built in the 1800s for $190,000? And I would only need a quarter of that much space. Thanks for the invite and I will definitely come visit, but it will be in the fall when all the trees are turning autumn colors in New England.

Speaking of unique places. . . I found a cottage in Normandy on craigslist that Anne is checking out for me. The wanderlust never ends, and I have no clue where I will travel when I leave Homer next fall.

After lunch we drive back to the Hangout Bar on the beach, and no, we are NOT having cocktails. Instead, we are looking for the Mexican guy with the beautiful silver jewelry for Juanita, who missed out last weekend and feels the need to buy more silver. She finds two incredible bracelets; actually, one is a string of silver beads that she wraps around her wrist three times. Her sisters also found silver bracelets that they had to have.

While the girls are shopping, I'm on the white sand beach looking at the incredible view of the bay with Stevie Nicks singing in the background. Can it get any better than this?

Chapter 40 – Rummaging at the Market, Again

Wednesdays are always great because we know that after workout, the market opens and is waiting for us. Juanita, her sister and brother-law, Jasmine, and I are looking forward to the treasure hunt. Oh no, only one guy with four women and we're going shopping? Does he know what he's in for? I doubt it.

It is such a hoot to go into the bowels of these outdoor tents and rummage through the racks and racks of stuff to find a perfect dress, skirt, blouse, shawl or whatever. Juanita and her sister are masters at it, and they just keep handing me things that are "so you." In the background, the husband is making snide comments about the fact we haven't missed a vendor on either side. Where else can you have this much fun for $20? Well, he had some suggestions . . . Never mind, he just doesn't get it.

I found so many treasures today—maybe because I am leaving for a couple weeks and have to stock up. Shopping is exhausting, so we stopped at Poncho Villa for chicken fajitas on the way home—always delicious, and the waiter remembers me. When I start giving my order, he says, *"Ensalada, right?"* I'm becoming a regular in Guaymas. The brother-in-law thought lunch was by far the best part of the day.

Over lunch, Jasmine tells us that she has lost another two kilos and her new diet plan for this week includes avocado and cheese sandwiches. We are in awe of this and can't believe it's true. We think she has read it wrong (it's in Spanish) because our diet specifically says NO avocado. Is she really going to the diet center, or is she confused and going some other place? I haven't had a piece of cheese, avocado or bread in over six weeks. And she gets it on her third week? Something is wrong with this picture.

On the way home we pass a Dairy Queen and Al, the brother-in-law, tells us if we work out for one hour on his Elliptical we can have an Oreo Cookie Blizzard. Supposedly you can burn 350 calories in one-half hour, and the blizzard has 700. Jasmine is very skeptical of these statistics and tells him so. Al becomes emphatic that this is the case and a funny argument ensues, ending with Al telling Jasmine to forget it; she would not be allowed to use his Elliptical after all. Are we obsessing over food?

We arrive back at Casa Miramar and find a houseful of people and sounds. The construction workers next door are using a jackhammer, the alarm system guy is doing an installation in the casa, the plumber is working to get the new fountain finished, and Maggie is sitting in the sun in the midst of all this, with ear plugs. The quiet abode that we left earlier today is alive with activity. We are happy to see Maggie, back from Copper Canyon with lots of stories and indigenous treasures, including a snake carved out of wood that looks a bit creepy.

A few hours later things are back to our natural rhythm at Casa Miramar. I fix the girls a rum and Coca Light and we sit on the back deck talking about traveling to Greece and the men in our lives, not necessarily in that order! The discussion leads us to a "pack pledge" that we toasted and shook on—we are NOT getting married. As Maggie said, *"What's the point at this stage of life?"*

I was inspired to photograph twice today —peeling paint at the market and kelp/seaweed on the beach. I have learned to take my inspiration when it comes because if I don't, the moment will pass and the inspiration fades

.

Chapter 41 – The Incredible Facial

Boot camp today was a longer run. I'm hangin' in there with running. Still waiting for that endorphin high that everyone talks about. We return to the casa to work on legs and our favorite abdominal crunches. I'm not complaining, it's definitely working!

It's time for another pampering day in San Carlos at Anna Marie's salon. First I get a much needed hair highlight of blonde and copper tones, and yes there was definitely running water here. There was also no need for me to fall off the chair to get their attention.

Next, we enter into the quiet room for the facials Juanita and I had booked early in the week. Soft music, luxurious chairs and the best facial ever! The esthetician actually opens the pores with steam and them cleans them with a tool that might be illegal in the U.S. And the neck and head massage? Wow! I think I nodded off for a while. My face feels so clean and is much softer than before. It lasted for an hour and a half and cost about $30.

They also do eyeliner/brow tattooing, plus a new procedure for the same that is a colored paint, no needles, that lasts 3-5 years. They offer the works—waxing, massages and just about anything else you can think of to pamper yourself. It's a good thing I'm leaving for Austin on Monday, or I would have booked more appointments.

Al invited Juanita, Maggie and I over to dinner at the beachfront house. He had prepared a delicious chicken dish. Juanita and I were tempted to lick our plates, it was so yummy. The chicken was simmered in a tomato sauce with interesting spices—it's been a long time since we've had anything but grilled pollo! Plus, Al had made three different salads to accommodate the diet plan. He really outdid himself and we so appreciated it.

We head back to the house for an early night in—and we did not stop at Froggies on the way! We saw Roger at the security guard station and stopped to say hi. Roger (a.k.a. Zesto) was a street dog that used to hang out at the guard station, and eventually got adopted by Cindy, an English teacher from Chicago. He loves his new home and is allowed to sit on the couch, bed, wherever. He is now treated like a dog should be, at least in my opinion. When he goes out during the day, he goes straight to the guard shack to resume his post. Roger, like many dogs, needs a job, and he has found one with the security guards. Rumor has it that they bring him fried liver for a treat, and what canine can resist that? Cindy is struggling with the decision to bring Roger back to Chicago when she leaves in May, or leave him here. That's a tough one! Roger loves his life as it is now.

One more day of boot camp and then we're off to Austin for yoga practice at Yoga Yoga for a week. I just found out that it's going to be SXSW (yearly film and music festival) while I'm in town. Another new experience!

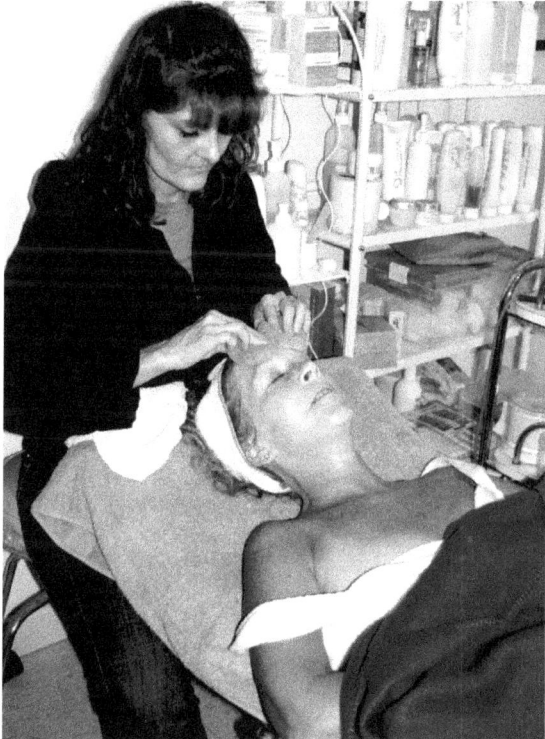

Chapter 42 – A Lip Massage?

We made it through our last day of boot camp, and I'm sure Antonio will miss our routine and us almost as much as we will miss him. The abdominals were intense and for my last set I counted 35 before I couldn't do another. Juanita is headed back to Seattle (and snow) to run the stair race, and I am going to Austin for the South By Southwest (SXSW) music fest and yoga practice. We are both returning to Guaymas in a couple weeks. Maggie will still have boot camp through Wednesday when she, too, will be returning to Vashon Island, hoping to be back to Mexico sometime in the summer.

My dental appointment was scheduled for this afternoon, but Jasmine and Dave called inviting Maggie and I to go out on their boat for the afternoon. That sounded like much more fun, so I canceled the dentist. Then, Juanita told me that she heard he was very good looking. Oh well, I already canceled. Maybe I will reschedule when I return from Austin.

We were out on the boat for approximately 30 minutes before we called it a day and returned to the harbor. The wind was really strong and Maggie and I got soaked in a matter of minutes, as we headed into the wind. So much for finding the dolphins. We made a date to try again at a later time. And I canceled my dental appointment to get wet?

Maggie had the bright idea to stop by the dental office to see if he could squeeze me in. So okay, we walk in the dental office wrapped in towels (remember, we are soaked) and ask if it was possible to reschedule now. The receptionist and hygienist did not look pleased with this request (they were ready to close) but insisted *"one moment,"* and made a phone call. In a matter of seconds an extremely handsome man appeared before us and invited me back to his office.

He proceeds to clean my teeth and tell me I have a beautiful face about three times. Okay, so it's a sales job, but it is working. His face is only inches from mine and I can hear him breathing as he works in my mouth. I am extremely nervous—attractive men do that to me. He finishes up by rubbing my cheeks and massaging my lips with lip-gloss. Now really, has anyone you know ever had their lips massaged after a teeth cleaning? It was awesome and unsettling. I got out of the chair to leave and my towel fell off! I am walking away desperately trying to cover up my bikini bottom. Smiling, he asked me if I might be going swimming again. I explained the boat ride from hell. I was babbling and I knew it! My teeth look great, I am rattled, and where was Maggie? I was so hoping for a picture of this experience, but she's nowhere around. Next time, and there definitely will be a next time. What is it with doctors lately?

Maggie had walked over to the bank, so we met up outside. The moment was gone and he had disappeared. He must live in the complex; otherwise, how could he have been there so quickly? I had to tell her about my dental experience over martinis! So we went to our favorite restaurant and had two. And she agreed, she has never had her lips massaged by a dentist either! They sure do things differently in Mexico—in a good way!

On the way home it occurred to me that I was in for sticker shock when I returned to the States. We had Bombay martinis for about $3 each. Almost as unbelievable as the lip massage!

Chapter 43 – Dinner With Gringos

Maggie, Juanita and I started the day with a hike to the shell beach. The trailhead is next to the oyster factory, where they actually farm oysters and create jewelry with the pearls. The hike was beautiful and we ended up on a remote beach with crystal clear water. And, the shells were stacked ankle deep! We found so many treasures to bring home.

I had an appointment at noon for OgDog to get a haircut. He is coming up on his 16th birthday and tires easily. I volunteered to help the vet with the grooming, which took about two hours. OgDog did really well in the beginning but got fussy toward the end, snapping at the vet and me. But that's OgDog, always speaking his mind. I ended up with his hair in my eyes, nose, ears, and even inside my bra. I have no idea how this happens, but every time I groom him, his hair manages to get inside all of my clothes. But it's nothing a hot shower can't fix. Grooming always makes him spunky and he is now ready for his trip to Austin.

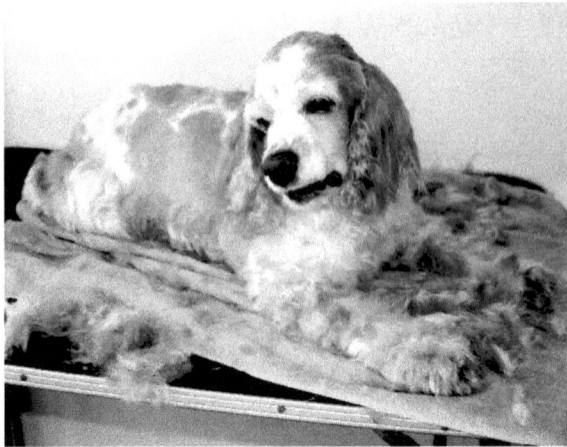

We have a dinner date with the gang tonight at La Conquista where I am now treated as a regular. I can't wait for the rib-eye that they do so well. Jasmine started the evening by "showing" us how much weight she had lost, based on how big her pants were. Okay, we get it. You're going to cheat tonight, right? Juanita decided on ONE martini even though her siblings wondered if it was a good idea since she was the "DD." We won't mention driving home after our night out at Froggies . . . no need to stir that pot.

After dinner someone announced that it was Al's birthday! Our waiter made a huge deal over this, including a complimentary dessert that looked fabulous. I didn't have any but I noticed many of my diet partners decided to have a taste. Al picked up the tab for all the dinners and drinks! Can you believe it? Thanks Al, but come on. It was YOUR birthday!

Or was it? A couple drinks, a great meal, good company and an early night for us girls. We have packing to do mañana. No Froggies for us tonight. We are going home early. It's a first!

Chapter 44 – Last Night in Guaymas

The last day in Guaymas included packing up the casita, cleaning VeVe, packing VeVe, and lying by the pool for breaks in between. I'm sad to leave but I will be back in a fortnight for another three weeks. Juanita left for Seattle at 5 a.m., and Maggie will be here until Thursday, when she will also return to the Pacific Northwest. We ended the day with a spaghetti dinner at the beachfront house. The host grilled burgers and topped them with scrumptious spaghetti sauce for the diet girls. There was a fresh green salad, garlic bread and a yummy dessert (apple/peach torte) that Maggie made. She used Splenda for the sweetener so we could eat the fruit out of the middle without the pastry. We passed on the French bread!

We said our Mexican goodbyes with hugs and kisses, promising to keep in touch. We were back at Casa Miramar and in bed by 9:30. I have a long day of driving out of Mexico mañana. Sigh. . . Tomorrow is Monday—and a trip to the diet center for weigh-in before I leave is a MUST!

Part III

North to the Border and SXSW

*"Travel doesn't become adventure until
you leave yourself behind"*
—Marty Ruben

Chapter 45 – The Adventure North

I am ready to hit the road at 8:30 a.m., so I take the dogs for one more beach walk, say goodbye to Maggie and drive to the diet center for weigh-in and two diet plans for my trip. I was so pleased when she said I had lost another kilo, and could not help but smile and say yippee! This week my diet plan is: cereal with light milk or two pieces of light toast with marmalade for breakfast; apple or pear for snack; vegetable soup and salad for lunch; and chicken, beef or fish with salad for dinner. Pretty simple.

Our trip to Nogales is quiet and takes about 4.5 hours. I will be in Tucson in early afternoon and should be able to make El Paso tonight. We are approximately one mile from the U.S. border when I hear a beep, look at the dash and see a bright RED light. Oh no, oil? I pull over immediately, cut the engine and get out the manual. It's not the oil light, but the temperature gage. VeVe is overheating and here we are barely off the freeway with little room to park. Yikes! Now what? I pop the hood and, sure enough, she is really hot. I start flagging people to stop. There are mostly trucks on the road and one going in the opposite direction actually stops, and a Mexican guy runs across the freeway with a jug of water to put in the reservoir. Somehow he knew the problem but our communication is limited. After filling the reservoir, he returned to his truck with a promise to send help.

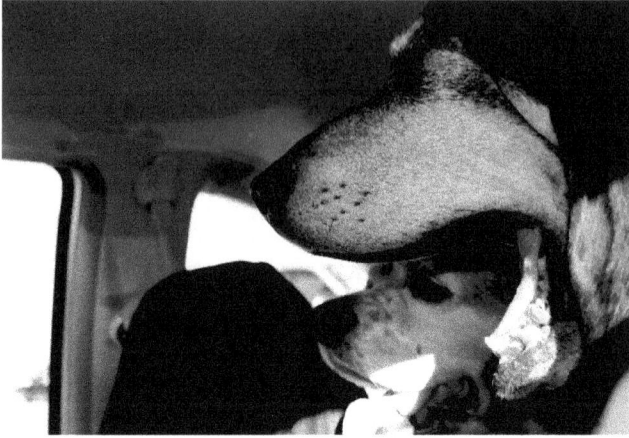

The dogs are panting and I am sweating as I continue stopping cars— interesting that the Americans pass me by but four Mexicans stop to help. I'm trying to tell them that I need a tow truck, but to no avail. One guy actually tried calling a tow company, but I couldn't understand what he said about that. Silly Woman should have done some Spanish homework!

In the meantime, we are sitting in the hot sun trying to figure out Plan B. I notice that just ahead there is a huge downhill run for about a mile. I turn VeVe on and cruise to the top of the incline, killing the engine and coasting down, gaining enough speed to get to the top of the other side. And then, the red light came on again. Once again I pull over. I am somewhere between Nogales, Sonora and Nogales, Arizona.

Finally, an Indian man stopped and he could speak English. He asked me how long the light had been red, and I told him I had turned off the engine immediately after the beep. He said the border was less than a mile and there was a Shell station directly on the other side. He thought I could make it without hurting anything if I would coast whenever possible and pull over if the red light came on again to let VeVe cool off—a long process since it is about 85 degrees.

But, what were my choices? I decided to take his advice and make a run for the border. Fortunately, the red light never came on so there was no need to pull over again. We made it to the border okay and ended up sitting in line for over two hours to cross. I had the engine off most of that time, starting it up only to move forward a few feet at a time. We finally cross the border and I arrive at the Shell station where a Mexican mechanic has a makeshift garage in a tent. Another language barrier, but basically he told me it was my water pump and it would be three days before he could get the part from Phoenix! THREE DAYS???? And Phoenix, why not Tucson?

I decided to call a tow truck for a quote—$250 to Tucson, about 60 miles. They told me that we would not arrive in Tucson before closing time so I should try to get it fixed here. Aye yi yi! I hung around (where was I going?) and asked the tent mechanic if he would rent me a car (I would go to Tucson and get the part); no, he couldn't do that. I will pay extra to get the part here quicker; no, that was not possible. Okay, so now what?

I think he was tired of my questions, so he finally said as he pointed to a truck that was in line for gas at the station: *"Do you want me to ask him to tow you to Tucson?"* Sure enough, the gas customer had an empty trailer on the back of his SUV. I said yes, please! He sprinted across the parking lot and came back saying the guy would be over to talk with me. I ask him if it was his amigo and he said no—a stranger with a trailer only. Wow, he just earned a huge tip!

The Mexican bilingual introduced himself as Gilbert. I

noticed he had three small children in the car with him—Nathan, Lelah, and Aden. He had just towed a car from Tucson to the border for a friend and was on his way home. He said he would be happy to help me but I had to ride in the front with him, and the dogs would have to stay in VeVe. I agreed, so we hooked up VeVe and the dogs to the trailer and I got in the front seat of his car. After we drove a couple miles it occurred to me that I'm in a car with a complete stranger and everything I own is in the car behind us.

Any doubts about our safety quickly dissolved. It turned out Gilbert was a single dad with three wonderful babies—they were the best. It is now 6 p.m. and the only thing I've had to eat today was cereal and I'm getting a little spacey from lack of food. We stopped at McDonald's. I got the kids and dogs burgers and me a grilled chicken salad.

We arrived in Tucson around 8 p.m., exhausted. Not only did Gilbert tow me to Tucson but he found us a dog-friendly Motel 6, unloaded VeVe, gave me his cell number and told me to call him in the morning and he would take me to a reasonable mechanic he knows! He also doesn't think I have a water pump problem since there was no coolant spewing out on the ground. His guess is the thermostat, a much easier thing to fix. Things are looking up!

The dogs and I are so happy to get to the motel. We went directly to bed and got up early to see the mechanic. Sure enough, it was my thermostat and not the water pump. Gilbert drove me to the auto parts store, I picked up the part that the mechanic had called in ($22), took it back to him, and he installs it in 20 minutes for $20! I am feeling very grateful today for this wonderful man who has gone out of his way to help us and for the mechanic and the easy fix on VeVe. Imagine if I had stayed in Nogales for the repair! I gave Gilbert a hug and had to insist he take $100. This experience has once again taught me that there are wonderful people out there to connect with. For some reason our paths were supposed to cross at this time, and I'm very thankful for that.

It's 9:30 a.m. and I'm ready to get on Highway 10 headed southeast to Austin. It's 850 miles so maybe I can make it tonight. At midnight my eyes are starting to cross and the lights ahead are getting blurry. We're only 139 miles west of Austin but I need sleep. No sooner had the thought entered my mind and I see: Motel 6 next exit! I always know my dogs will be welcome there. It's been a long day but we're smilin'.

Chapter 46 – Austin & Yoga Yoga

The dogs and I arrive in Austin early morning. . .the last 139 miles of the trip took us through Texas Hill Country. It was a cool morning with bright sunshine that warmed the air to a nice 70-plus degrees by noon. Springtime in the Hill Country means the trees and flowers are in bloom. The highlight of the drive was Fredericksburg, a small town with many eclectic shops and restaurants to explore. Close by is Enchanted Rock State Park, a mystical, spiritual place with great hiking trails. We passed through very early so most places were still closed.

We are happy to be in Austin where the people are friendly and the weather is fabulous! I went to Central Market to get my food for the week. With the diet plan, shopping is simple! I love Central Market—so much good produce (from Mexico), and organic choices. However, it is expensive! I knew I would be in sticker-shock after leaving Mexico; glad it's Texas because Washington and Alaska will be an even bigger shock when I return in May!

Yoga Yoga is next door to the market so I bought a weekly pass and will start tomorrow. They offer classes from 7 a.m. to 7 p.m. every day, and the choices are incredible: Hatha, Hatha Flow, Kundalini, Restorative, Relaxation and Breathing

Techniques —just about any non-trendy yoga you can think of is offered at Yoga Yoga. I could stay in Austin just for the yoga community alone.

My friend Sue and I had a late lunch at Cheddars—a small chain with good steaks and salads. It's an early night for me. After a couple gin and tonics on the deck, the dogs and I are hitting the sack. SXSW Film Festival ends today and the music starts tomorrow. It's nice to be in Austin, but I do miss the Guaymas lifestyle and my friends there! The fashion is a bit different here. Should I get some boots to go with my treasures from the Guaymas market? That would surely put me in Texas style. But, I'm really not the cowgirl type!

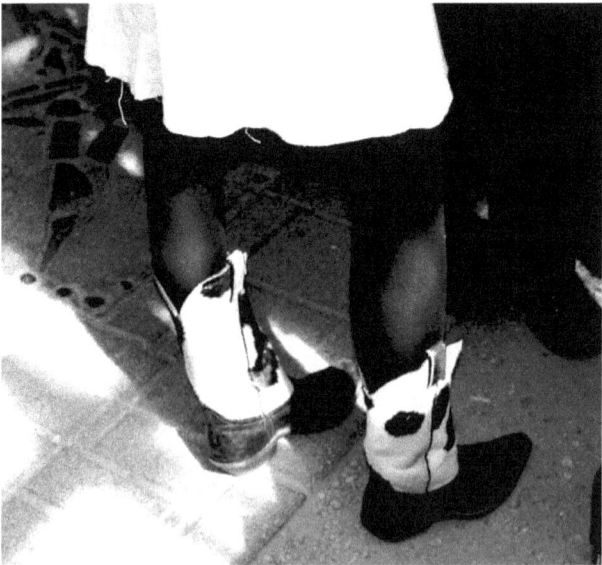

Chapter 47 – Maintaining the Regimen

I started my day by running. YES, running—Antonio would be proud. I'm doing that part of boot camp while I'm in Austin. Sue and her springer spaniel JJ came along on the bike. The weather was cool in the morning and perfect for running a few blocks. And running on pavement is definitely easier than the beach sand, but obviously not as gorgeous. I followed up by taking the dogs for a walk around the neighborhood. They had major sniffing and peeing to do in the new area.

Kundalini yoga is a physical and meditative discipline, comprising a set of techniques that use the mind, senses, and body to create a communication between mind and body. Kundalini yoga focuses on psycho-spiritual growth and the body's potential for maturation, giving special consideration to the role of the spine and the endocrine system in the understanding of yogic awakening. This class at Yoga Yoga was amazing—I remember the instructor from last year.

We worked on neutral mind with breathing techniques designed to energize and relax the body. One of the standing poses was closing your eyes and holding your mouth like you're whistling, blowing in and out with your arms extended overhead. It's about concentrating on the sound you're making and tuning in to the sound the rest of the room is making, simultaneously. By doing so, you stay in the present moment.

And the GONG! I am totally addicted to it! For the final relaxation pose, Savasana, we lay on our back, eyes closed, shoulders tucked under, feet relaxing out, and hands at our sides, facing up. The yogi hits the gong softly at first, building intensity over a 10-minute period. I feel the reverberation through my entire body, mind and spirit. We were warned that once we got up from this relaxation, it would feel like being drunk. Sure enough, I staggered out of class, spilling my chai tea that was given out after the session—and I swear I had nothing to drink before 10 a.m. this morning. It's such a terrific feeling that you find yourself with a perpetual smile on your face. This is an amazing experience that everyone should have at least once, but it is addictive. Did I mention I could stay in Austin for the yoga community alone?

Sue and I spent the afternoon looking at the SXSW schedule and selecting bands to see. I saw that Tim Easton, an Alaska musician, was playing at Maria's Taco Xpress tomorrow. Bands are playing all over town at various restaurants and bars. Each one plays approximately 25 minutes and then they rotate and another one hits the stage. It sounds like a great time. Sue is headed to Denton tomorrow for a seminar, so I'm on my own. I called Donna, another friend here, and made plans to meet at Maria's taco joint tomorrow afternoon for live music and food.

Today we decided on a matinee, "Slumdog Millionaire," at the Westgate Center. The story, the actors, the music, everything was so well done. I was blown away with the filming techniques, and can certainly see why it won the Oscar. I don't think I said a word the entire movie, and that has to be a first for me! The soundtrack is also amazing and one I will be adding to my collection. Can you tell I liked it?

We grilled out this evening—chicken breasts and fresh asparagus (again from Mexico), along with a few Bacardi Cuba Libres. Yummy! Still no wine, still no cerveza, and still maintaining the diet plan—it's been seven weeks. Life is good for a Silly Woman and four perros in Austin!

Chapter 48 - SXSW

Keeping with the program, I went for a run this morning and then to a Hatha yoga class that was really tough. I really should look at the class level before just showing up. But I do think I'm pretty good at this by now, but this instructor was all about difficult poses and holding them for five breaths! It was the hand and headstands that put me over the edge, especially after trying to balance my body weight on my elbows. Whatever! I just stuck with my usual shoulder stand and faded into the back of the room. Jeez, will I ever get this balancing thing down? I guess I could give up the Cuba Libres for a night and see if that helps. How boring is that?

Donna picked me up for the afternoon and we headed over to South Lamar to Maria's Taco Xpress—it was PACKED! People everywhere—in Sin City Social Club, in the restaurant, in line to order food, at the bar to get beers. No place to sit and hardly any place to stand. We got in the food line, placed our order and Donna told me to find a table and she would pick up the fajitas. BTW, they didn't hold a candle to the chicken fajitas at Poncho Villa in Guaymas! I walked around the patio area and saw a couple clearing their table, asked if they were leaving and they were not, but offered me a couple chairs to sit with them. I scored! Just a smile and a question got us a great seat!

We were just in time to catch Tim Easton, an Alaskan musician. He put on a great show and the crowd loved his music. A couple more girls from Houston joined our table and everyone continued rotating in and out of Sin City— a constant flow of people in cowboy boots. Since we had such a good seat, we stayed for the next four shows and had multiple table partners.

There was a guy one table over who resembled Robin Williams. When he got up I noticed he was wearing a short skirt that cracked me up. As he passed by our table I got out the camera to get a shot from behind and just when I got it focused he turned around and caught me. We both laughed and he offered to pose, but first he pulled his skirt down on the side to show me his lace underwear. Hilarious! And this sounds like something Robin Williams would actually do, right? It was very crowded so I could not get anything but a close-up shot of his skirt and the lace, a little out of focus, but you get the picture. Many people were in costume; I should have worn my carnival mask and invited Juanita!

All the bands were really good. A country group called The

Stone River Boys certainly looked like they were from the '50s, but their music was fun and upbeat. One of the lead singers looked exactly like Roy Orbison with sunglasses. I loved his ducktail hairstyle—I think that's what it's called when hair is long and slicked back on both sides?

Susan Marshall is a jazzy blues singer that was exceptionally talented with a voice like Aretha Franklin. We had a great time listening to the diverse music presented at Maria's. When we finally did leave, we drove through downtown Austin and SOCO, south of Congress. People were lined up in the streets and traffic was jammed. A bike would have made much better sense. There were so many outdoor bars and cafés with loud music and dancing crowds, but you can only do so much in one day. We headed home so I could feed the dogs, all five of them since JJ is with me while Sue is in Denton.

Tomorrow is another day and we will once again hit the streets in search of more SXSW music!

Chapter 49 - More SXSW

This was a weekend full of entertainment and good food. After my morning run, a doggie walk, and a relaxing yoga session, we went to Sixth Street in downtown Austin. Anyone familiar with Austin probably knows this as the eclectic, funky, hippy, alternative area of town. You can get a tattoo, massage, hear a country song, see people playing music on the street, get a beer or just window shop. We actually "bar" shopped, spending the day in and out of dark places to catch some music. Band after band. . . I'm curious whether this is a juried festival or if the bands simply pay money to attend. There are record company agents floating through the crowds looking for fresh talent, and many private parties. We did ask one lead singer how to get in, and she admitted her band got in by knowing someone. Apparently, SXSW is as political as most organized events.

We had lunch at the Pecan Street Café on Sixth—rib-eye salad and a Cuba Libre. I can't have wine, so I settle for Bacardi with my steak. Apparently, Sixth Street was formerly named Pecan Street, so this café has been around for some time. We were not allowed access to the upstairs because of a private party. If Juanita had been with me, I'm sure she would have talked our way in the door.

Speaking of Juanita. . . she called today to say that she was doing the run on Sunday, up the stairs in Seattle—69 floors. Yikes! Good luck, girly, and it's a good thing it's only 30 degrees there. Doing that in Guaymas could cause a heat stroke about now. And the bad news. . . Juanita will not be back in Mexico for a few months. So when I return next week I will be on my own with the exception of Mike from Anchorage, who will be visiting for a week, followed by Chad and his family for another week. It will then be time for me to start my trek back to the Greatland. While I was talking to Juanita on the phone, Margaret (no more Maggie) arrived back on Vashon. I'm sure she's in a snit about the cold weather that welcomed her back to the island. Hang in there, girlfriend. Spring is coming!

Sunday we spent the afternoon in another colorful Austin neighborhood, SOCO. I would classify this area as the art district. Most of the bands were playing in outside cafés and there were many artists selling their wares at the Street Fair. We stopped on the way home to get a flavor of the redneck bars starting with the Saxon Pub—it was so dark in there I could not see my hand in front of my face. Yikes! But the band was really good! One quick drink and we're out of there. We ended the day with a pit stop at The Broken Spoke—the name says it all. The crowd looked us up and down, like aliens! No band here until 7:30, only beady eyes checking us out. We're not hangin' out here for long; it feels very awkward. Another quick drink and we're out of there.

On the way home I had to stop at a department store to get face cream and mascara. Boy, was I surprised when I walked out of Scarborough's with a vibrator—yes, that's right. Mascara with a vibrator on the wand. Can you believe it? You actually put the brush to your lashes, push a button on the side and it vibrates the mascara onto your lashes —supposedly lifting and separating. That just cracked me up so I had to have it. Can you imagine? I'm going to give it a try and, at the cost of $34, it better work. Jeez, what will they will come up with next?

SXSW will officially end tonight. Sad, but I am exhausted. Same time, same place next year.

Chapter 50 - Eating, Drinking And Yoga

It's 35 degrees in Austin this morning! There was a blizzard last night (as in snow) just north of here, near Amarillo. I am delaying my run this morning until around 9:30 or 10, letting the sun warm up the air first. Jeez, it's freezing right now.

I have spent the week immersing myself in both Hatha and Kundalini yoga, running a mile-plus each morning, and walking the dogs about the same distance. I have weigh-in next week in Guaymas so then I will know if it was worth giving up all the Tex-Mex food that surrounds me.

I scored at the Austin Goodwill again—a sexy camisole, two pairs of casual capri pants, and a glittery, tight, hot pink T-shirt. Glittery? Well, it's the Mexico influence. Love this thrift store shopping; however, the prices are not as good here as the Guaymas market, where I will return soon for still more treasures. While in the shopping mode, I am oblivious to how much I have collected over the winter. But I do know I have a closet full in Mexico and another closet full in Vashon. Yikes! Now the question is: How am I going to get all these clothes back to Homer, and just what am I going to do with them? I know it's an art project and I also know it's a website for upcycling. But that's all I know at this point. BTW, I returned the vibrator. You know the one attached to the mascara wand? It didn't work all that well and it was $34—that's a day of shopping at the Goodwill!

Lots of good food places in Austin. The Hyde Park Grill next to Yoga Yoga has been a hangout for me. Yummy burgers and organic salads. For the price, Cheddars has been a standby for sirloin steaks—$11.95 and they are good! I had my first Mexican martini at El Mercado's, one of my favorite Mexican restaurants here. A Mexican martini is tequila (duhh), olive juice, lime juice and Grand Marnier, making it a bit sweet. For my second one I asked they just use a half-shot of the Grand Marnier so it was more tart. I had only two with my chicken taco salad minus the guacamole, cheese and sour cream. Actually, the salad was chicken, lettuce, and tomatoes—not hardly a taco salad, I guess. I also had my usual four chips broken into pieces for dipping small bites in salsa. Getting in shape has major sacrifices, but it's all good.

Thunderstorms have been happening for the last couple of days. It gets really dark, lightning streaks the sky and then a loud clatter marks the beginning of torrential rains that last maybe an hour or two. Then the sun comes out and quickly dries everything, leaving no evidence that it ever rained!

We saw "Grand Torino" with Clint Eastwood. The movie touched on racism, overcoming differences, friendship and mortality. The ending was a surprise, not unusual for an Eastwood flick. And, he played an excellent crochety old man.

I received word that a friend and colleague of mine lost her battle with breast cancer on Thursday night. It was a shock to all of us, as we had no idea she was even close to the end. Debbie was a wonderful, good soul and will be missed by all who knew her. Another reminder that life is often short and definitely needs to be "lived" while we have it.

Time for a run. Antonio would definitely be proud of me. Hopefully it's warmer than 35 degrees by now!

Part IV

South to the Border & Guaymas

"Traveling - It leaves you speechless,
then turns you into a storyteller"
- Battuba

165

Chapter 51 – On the Road Back

Monday morning and we are ready to hit the road AGAIN. The dogs and I spent Sunday afternoon getting VeVe ready for our departure from Austin. It's tricky getting all the les trés jours packed in such a way that a dog bed can fit on top, and three dogs are comfortable in the back, while OgDog sits in the passenger seat. We said our goodbyes to Yoga Yoga, the neighborhood, Sue, and the two doggies I cared for this weekend—JJ and Waylon Jennings. Austin is a wonderful city, but I don't want to buy a house here like I once thought. Visiting is just fine.

Clarity. . . . Once I stop trying to control my life and just live it, amazing things happen. I have been searching for a "place" to call my base for a couple years now. It finally occurred to me that I cannot leave Alaska—it will always be my base and I can just travel out of there. I want to simplify things and buying another house is not simple. When I do decide to buy another place, it will be in Europe and I will wait until that time is right. So, I will live in Homer this summer and run TBTB Dog Camp, and then in the fall move to my condo in Anchorage. It's been a few years since I have actually lived in Anchorage and it's a wonderful city. Plus, I will be living right downtown where I can walk to restaurants, museums, galleries, and theatres. My family will only be 42 miles north, and the airport is less than 15 minutes away. So when the dark, snow, cold get to me, I can hop a plane to Guaymas to see Juanita, or Seattle to see my friends there, or even Hawaii! And no more trips down the Alaska Highway for this Silly Woman in the near future! Life is good.

Driving through west Texas today was windy and dusty. We stopped at a rest area and all the dogs got burrs imbedded in their paws. When I tried pulling them out, they got stuck in my fingers. To be so small, those bastards really hurt. I won't miss this part of Texas, nor will the doggies. I do love the 80 mph speed limit on Highway 10. BTW, on the road to Austin, I got stopped for speeding at night. After dark the speed limit reduces to 65 for both cars and trucks. After taking lessons from Juanita in Guaymas on how to get out of a ticket, I applied her techniques of explaining myself nonstop in this situation, and it worked! He only gave me a warning.

Highway 10 just goes and goes, with a beautiful landscape but no services. It was getting a little scary when the gas gauge dropped below the reserve line. Driving 80 mph really eats the petrol up quickly and the gas stations were few and far between, like Alaska can be. Fortunately, we were able to coast into an Exxon station in the nick of time, filled up VeVe's tank, and were good to go for another 400-plus miles.

I am happy to report that we are at dog-friendly Motel 6 in Las Cruces, New Mexico. Our trip to Tucson will be short tomorrow, about 250 miles. We will spend the night there and leave early in the morning for Guaymas. We should arrive at the casita by 3 p.m. where Antonio will be waiting with the keys and information on how the new alarm system works.

We're almost back to the diet doctor, the piercing doctor, the facial salon, chicken fajitas at Poncho Villa, the market, the beach, the sunsets, and La Conquista martinis! Can you tell I've missed Guaymas?

Chapter 52 – The Good Sleep

It is wonderful to be back in Guaymas. I fully expected to stay in Tucson tonight, but then realized I had gained two hours coming from Austin. At noon, I saw the sign that said Tucson 80 miles, and wondered what I was going to do there for the whole afternoon. Why not make a run for Mexico? I AM a driving maniac.

I called Juanita and she contacted Antonio to see if he would be available to be there between 6-7 p.m. with the keys. No problem, everything was a GO for me to continue into Mexico and make Casa Miramar before dark. And, the good news? It doesn't get dark until 7 now. So the dogs and I were off on our marathon run back to our casita. The instructions were: no whining and we were not stopping until we reached our destination—five hours away.

We passed over the international border around 2 p.m. In usual doggie form, the pack went to sleep and didn't wake up until they sensed we were almost home. The speed limit is posted at 100 kmh, or 60 mph. I have learned that you follow the speed on the road, always behind someone going faster. I drove 80 mph most of the way, and a car with California license plates passed us like we were standing still.

We pulled into Guaymas at 10 minutes after 7. Please, Antonio, wait for us! By the time we reached Casa Miramar, it was closer to 7:30, but the gates were open, the lights were on, the doors were unlocked, and Antonio was waiting with hugs for all. What a nice welcome! I had to insist on driving him home; he was going to take the bus. But, I had to go to the grocery to get a few things since I hadn't eaten all day. He finally agreed to a ride since I was going out anyway.

I didn't realize how tired I was until I got into the Guaymas traffic and my eyes went blurry. Where was everyone going at 8 p.m. on a Tuesday? I managed to get Antonio home, and then stopped at the market to grab a few things. I wandered around aimlessly in the crowd, looking for cereal, milk, salad (sold out), ground beef (sold out), and eggs. When I got to the checkout, I realized it was just like that Sunday when I first arrived back in February. The lines were all very long, some over 10 shoppers deep with full baskets. And it's Tuesday night close to 9 p.m. I had the incredible urge to run out the door, but I had so much time already invested in getting this stuff, and there was nothing to eat in the casita. I was feeling very frazzled (probably from lack of food for the day) when a friendly Mexican lady walked up to me and said in perfect English that lane 11 was 10 items or less. Muchas gracias.

When I got to Lane 11 I saw that it was long and found myself wading through the clothes racks to find the end of this line—feeling more tempted than ever to bolt. Okay, breathe deeply; you are now in Mexico so enjoy the experience. That's what I had to say to myself to keep from running. And it was truly amazing to look around and see that nobody seemed in a hurry or frustrated about the lines. Finally, I settled in and waited like everyone else, making sure I did it with a smile on my face. It took about 15 minutes to check out, and then I was on my way home.

I passed a McDonald's on the left and thought about stopping for a grilled chicken salad to go, only to realize I would have difficulty getting my order understood, so the heck with it. I just want to be in the casita with the dogs and I can make do with the food I just bought.

I fed the dogs, put the groceries away, checked my email, unpacked, and had a bowl of cereal for dinner. By this time the doggies are stretched out across the bed and it's close to 11 p.m. I'm exhausted but glad to be home. Time for the good sleep that I always have in Mexico—doors open, breeze blowing through the house and the familiar neighborhood sounds.

Tomorrow morning is weigh-in. I've followed the diet closely, but what if I actually gained weight in Austin from all the Cuba Libres? The scales will soon tell.

Chapter 53 - Guaymas In The Spring

The bougainvillea and jasmine are in full bloom at Casa Miramar. It's amazing how much they have grown in the short time we were away. It is spring in Mexico.

The dogs and I took our usual morning walk on the beach and saw swimmers and snorkelers in the ocean for the first time. Apparently, the water has warmed up. Rather than doing a morning run, I got dressed and went to the diet center for weigh-in. My usual dietician was off today, so I saw a new consultant. Stepping on the scale was scary, but she told me I had lost a kilo—WHAT? Only one? She said that was really good, and then I realized—it had only been nine days since last weigh-in. It felt like I had been away for weeks! Okay, so I certainly can't complain about another kilo. I'm almost at my goal. With all this weight loss, my butt has headed south. OMG, maybe I need to find a plastic surgeon that does butt jobs. Or, have Antonio hold a butt boot camp by the pool.

She did the usual acupressure zaps—three on each side today, and the laser gun to the tummy area. She then turned on a machine that looked and sounded like a hand-held vacuum cleaner with rollers on the bottom that she placed on my tummy for a mini-massage. Not sure what that does, but it sure felt good! She gave me a diet plan for the new TWO weeks, because the office is going to be closed for Holy Week.

For Mexico, Easter is a combination of Semana Santa (Holy Week—Palm Sunday to Easter Saturday) and Pascua (Resurrection Sunday until the following Saturday). For most Mexicans, this two-week period is the time of year for vacation. It sounds like a good time to stay off the highways. I'm told that driving in San Carlos is out of the question during this time—it may take two hours to go one block. Glad for the heads-up on this one. My diet plan for the next two weeks consists of: cereal with light milk or yogurt with fresh fruit for breakfast; chicken (no beef), fish, fruits with the exception of bananas, mango, avocado and grapes, and any green vegetable. By now, I'm used to this.

After weigh-in, it's always time for lunch and I know just the place. But wait, the parking lot is empty? Then I saw the sign and remembered—they actually were in the process of moving the last time I was here. So I made a quick U-turn on the freeway and found their new location a few miles back. I love the Dorado or mahi-mahi, served with a green salad and my usual lemonada con gas.

It's now time for a siesta by the pool. The dogs love it and so do I. We are resting up because Mike arrives tomorrow afternoon and we know what that means—eating, drinking and partying, Mexican style. So what else is new?

Chapter 54 – Dancing With the Stars

The dogs and I took our morning walk and then it was time for my beach run—it's been awhile. The sand on the beach is so much harder to run on than the pavement in Austin. But I managed to get it done without stopping once. I guess you could say Antonio has made a runner out of me—a slow one but nevertheless I am running.

I have a few hours before getting Mike at the airport, so I settled in my recliner, poolside. It feels good to be back in the sunshine. I touched base with Jasmine and Dave and we decided on dinner tonight at 6. After a relaxing morning, I showered and headed to the bank for pesos and then to the Guaymas airport to pick up the next visitor to Casa Miramar. The plane was due in at 3:20 and I pulled into the parking lot early at 3:05. Imagine my surprise to see Mike standing next to his luggage waiting for me. Was I late? No, they were just 30 minutes early! Must have been a hellavu tail wind. There were only three people on the flight!

We put the luggage in the back of VeVe and headed off to find the nearest beverage joint—which wasn't all that far. Mike and I caught up over a couple cocktails and planned the rest of the day. We arrived back at the casa and got him settled into his room, freshened up and headed over to Jasmine and Dave's for cocktails. These guys are headed back to Boise on Tuesday. It's hard to believe that it's getting close to the time when all of us will head home. Already? Didn't I just get here?

We selected La Palapa for dinner—an outdoor restaurant with lots of great seafood and a table on the beach at sunset. Can it get any better than this? The server told us they would be closed the following week for Semana Santa. Really? This must be a huge event. Apparently, the beaches will be lined with campers having a good time—lots of drunken college kids with no money for dining in restaurants. And the traffic is so bad that it is hard for the staff to get to work, so many restaurants will be closed for the entire week. Okay, so I guess we're staying in Guaymas next week. But I have to find a way to get over there to photograph at least once before it's over. Sounds like the American version of spring break in Fort Lauderdale, but in Mexico they are celebrating the end of Lent and Holy Week.

On the way back to Jasmine and Dave's we passed Bananas on the corner and heard Mexican music pulsating through the walls. We had to stop. The scene was gringos drinking, dancing and having a blast. The true dancers in our group could not contain themselves. Jasmine and Mike hit the floor almost immediately, and eventually had Dave and I on our feet as well. We had so much fun. Who needs to run tomorrow morning after all this exercise? Mike was recruited as a "ringer" for a softball game in San Carlos tomorrow morning. He warned them that it was been years since he has played, but he was once awesome. We'll see. Will he even make it after all this dancing? We met the owner of the bar on our way out and promised to return soon.

Mike had a truly fine first day in Mexico. More fun and activities are planned for tomorrow. Stay tuned for all the gory details.

Chapter 55 – A Dog Named Luke

After all that dancing last night, running was easy this morning. Turns out the softball game is tomorrow morning and not today. So, when I got back to the casita after the beach run, we enjoyed a leisurely morning hanging out by the pool, reading, napping, and having breakfast outside in the beautiful sunshine. Mike needed to exchange some money for pesos so we went to the bank in San Carlos, stood in line for awhile and when it was our turn the guy in front of us turned and said we needed a copy of our passport to get money, grumbling something about being in line for so long and still not getting any money. He was not a happy camper – major attitude.

I told Mike I would exchange the money because he didn't have his passport with him. I went to the window and she said she needed a copy of my passport. I did my usual blonde blank look and said I didn't know where to get one, so she pointed next door. In the meantime, she counted out the pesos and went in the back with my passport, returning with a copy for her records. Whew! That was nice; now we don't have to go next door and then get back in the bank line. Muchas, muchas gracias! Being blonde has many advantages.

When we went outside, Hank the Crank was waiting for us,

wanting to know if they had given us pesos. When we said yes, he started bitching saying he would never come back to this bank. Maybe if he changed his perspective they might be more inclined to help him. Or maybe he could lighten his hair? Americans with attitudes in foreign countries can be so embarrassing!

The jewelry vendors had their wares spread out in front of the bank. I bought a gorgeous multi-colored bracelet for 40 pesos (under $3). While I was in the bank parking lot a vegetable vendor told us to come by his truck and he would give us a deal on fresh fruits and vegetables. True to his word, we bought fresh-squeezed OJ and grapefruit juice, and ripe tomatoes. The total was under $5, and he threw in a bunch of asparagus, two zucchinis, and a garlic head for free! People are so nice in Mexico.

Mike was interested in going on a fishing charter, so we inquired at Jon Jens Charters at the marina. It's too early for the marlin and Dorado, but they have been catching yellow fin, so Mike booked an early morning charter for Sunday. In the meantime, I fell in love with Luke, the golden retriever mascot—14 years old and adorable. He ran out and picked up a large rock in his mouth and brought it back to me—once a retriever, always a retriever. I'll bring Mike back at 6:30 a.m. any day just so I can see Luke again. What a great dog!

There was a bar on the rooftop of the marina hotel and it looked like a good place for lunch. Walking over there, we met a guy on a bike from Ketchikan, Alaska. What a small world! The restaurant had a spectacular view of the marina with Mt. Teta Kawi as the backdrop. Mike ordered marlin tacos; he can't catch them, so he might as well eat them in a restaurant. I had my usual grilled chicken and ensalada, but I did taste the yummy marlin.

Back to Guaymas and Supermercado Ley (my favorite grocery store, NOT) for booze, because it is cheap! Mike bought tequila, wine, vodka, and beer. Jeez, he must be planning on drinking a lot in a few days? I guess I will be forced to help out. We came back to the house for a couple of drinks, eventually walking to La Playa Del Cortes Hotel for a late dinner. We had a very full day and were both exhausted after we finished eating. We headed home for an early night because Mike is the ringer tomorrow for softball and he has to be on his game!

Chapter 56 – A Date with a Golden Retriever

The softball game in San Carlos started at 10 a.m. on a beautiful morning with high sun and a light breeze—perfect weather, not a cloud in the sky. Mike got right back into his game and was invited to play again on Tuesday. I sat on the sidelines talking to other expats (mostly Canadians) who spend their winters here—and taking pictures. Both teams played well but no one felt the need to keep score. It was about getting some exercise and having fun.

We walked over to the Soggy Peso beach bar afterwards for lunch. I had a melted tuna sandwich, less the cheese, and Panini bread—guess you could say I had tuna on a plate! It's on the diet, and I am committed to watching what I eat. I washed it all down with two Cuba Libras, unlike the beer drinkers in our crowd. Just enough sun, exercise and food to make me sleepy!

On the way home we stopped at my favorite market, Santa Rosa. When we came out I was surprised to see a little Mexican man washing VeVe. He had a Coke bottle and a rag, so I asked him what he was using on the car. He took a drink out of the bottle and said it's only agua—maybe he thought I wouldn't believe him? Anyhow, there were tons of bugs on her front hood from our Texas trip, so I was delighted to see that he had removed them with plain water, a soft rag and lots of elbow grease. Muchas gracias, señor—VeVe really appreciates being clean! I handed him some pesos and saw a young mother with her beautiful baby girl outside the market. I took their picture and offered some pesos for baby food—she was so appreciative.

Mike and I eventually ended up poolside for some sun and a quick nap. We are meeting the gang at Poncho Villa for a late dinner, and a walk around Town Square. As usual, the food was delicious and we had the waiter snap some pictures of us in front of a wall-sized picture of the legendary rebel general of the Mexican Revolution. After dinner we walked over to the boardwalk by the water and back through the city streets, passing a church where there was a coming-out celebration for several 15-year-old girls—similar to a debutant event. The dresses were incredible! Observation: Mexican women dress more feminine and much sexier than American women.

Mike has an early-morning fishing charter—I'm not interested in going! Killing fish is not my idea of a good time, but I do like to eat them. Does that make me a hypocrite or just someone not wanting to watch them die? But, I will take

Mike to San Carlos at 6 a.m. because I have a date with a golden retriever named Luke. Now that's my idea of a good time!

Chapter 57 – More Eating & Drinking. . .

Mike got out with Jon Jens fishing charter at 7 a.m. Fortunately he caught a 25-pound yellowfin straight away, because they ended up towing a stranded boat and crew into the harbor right after that, cutting the fishing time in half. The yellowfin will be filleted and vacuum packed for pick-up later. We took enough with us for dinner and some extra to pass on to Jasmine and Dave. We fired up the patio grill and cooked the fillets with some fresh asparagus, poolside. It's hard to say what tasted better—the fish or the asparagus. And the drinks were pretty good too.

The next couple of days are a blur—we were either lying by the pool reading, drinking, telling stories, eating, or napping. Other times we were shopping in San Carlos or downtown Guaymas, eating lunch at Los Barcos, or saving ourselves for dinner at Blackies. Whatever we were doing, it was a relaxing time because we did it with naptime by the pool and a beverage or two, in between activities. Time spent on the streets of downtown Guaymas was interesting. It is a busy, eclectic city, buzzing with activity. I totally got into street photography, even with the sun high in the sky, causing high contrast in the images.

Jon Jens offered Mike another morning of fishing at a reduced rate. After some contemplation, he decided to go—it's not every day you can fish in Mexico, and it IS a guy thing. So once again I'm up at 6 a.m. to drive him to the San Carlos marina. Not a problem, because Luke will be happy to see me. After dropping Mike off and hanging out with Luke for awhile, I came back to the casa, took the dogs to the beach for a walk, and then went for a run. The rest of the morning was spent poolside reading "The Instruction – How to Live the Life Your Soul Intended."

Mike enjoyed his time on the water but returned without catching any more fish. Oh well; apparently it wasn't meant to be. At least he didn't have to worry about getting fish back to Alaska—that's one way of looking at it. And he was on the water for the morning, which is a good thing. The good news? I got a free Jon Jens T-shirt for just hanging out.

It is Mike's last night in Mexico so I suggested dinner at La Conquista for the best rib-eyes around, not to mention the Bombay Sapphire martinis that are so cold you can see the ice crystals! These are guaranteed to make Mike forget about the Mexican fish that got away!

Chapter 58 – Ghosts at the Casa?

We have lots of feral cats in the neighborhood. Juanita had a large bag of cat food that I have been doling out in the evening, along with large bowls of fresh water—they seem very thirsty and have actually tried drinking the salt water out of the swimming pool. Finding fresh water has to be difficult for homeless animals.

We feed them on the wall next to the pool, high enough up so the dogs can't reach them. Luce is extremely curious, like she was with LeRoy, the cat on Vashon. She is content just to watch them and they don't seem to mind her being there. One day I went out to find her and a kitty by the pool, staring at each other—mesmerized, until the cat saw me and freaked.

I walked out of my bedroom this morning to find a little black cat on my kitchen counter by the sink. When she saw me, she jumped up the window trying to escape—limes went flying everywhere, scaring her even more. When that didn't work, she lunged onto the floor and flew out the door. She had to be so hungry to come in a house with four perros! They were sound asleep and heard nothing. Some watch dogs, huh? More food, that's what she was telling me.

Something else very strange happened this morning. The

fountain in the garden that had been shut off was running and soapsuds were spewing out of it—entering the twilight zone. I emailed Juanita because Antonio is not here today and I have no idea where the switch is, or why it is running. And, the soapsuds??? Poltergeist: a ghost that manifests itself by noises, rappings, and the creation of disorder. I've heard a few stories about definite ghostly experiences here at Casa Miramar. However, this feels okay, just a little strange but not in a bad way.

When Mike got up, he asked me if I heard the cat fight last night. Guess I went to sleep when my head hit the pillow because I didn't hear anything. Juanita called to tell me where the switch for the fountain was located. Guess where? On the wall directly below where the kitty bowls were AND, when I went to shut it off, all the bowls had been knocked to the ground. Maybe the cats were fighting over the food and either fell off the wall or jumped up on the wall and tripped the switch. That's a likely scenario as to why the fountain was running, but still does not explain the bubbles in the water. It's still a mystery.

Too much activity already this beautiful, sunny morning and it is caliente—the temperature has escalated the last few days. I ran on the beach and was drenched with sweat when I got home at 8 a.m. Mike and I decided a swim in the pool and a leisurely morning in the recliners was a better idea than the Wednesday market—much too hot to be on pavement with hordes of other people, shopping. I can't believe I'm saying this.

All Mike needed was a small cooler for the yellow fin that we could get on the way to the airport. After a lazy morning by the pool we have one last lunch at Poncho Villa after a stop at Woolworth's (it still exists in Mexico) for the cooler. I wanted to send Mike off with a tummy full of authentic enchiladas pollo de mole. His flight to Phoenix left at 3:50 p.m. It has been a truly fine week of relaxation, dancing, eating and drinking – not necessarily in that order. I can't believe it went by so fast. I now have two days to rest before the next group arrives at Casa Miramar—my son Chad and family Natasha and Zachary, along with mother-in-law Debbie and brother-in-law Jeremy. Their visit will be here for the week of spring break, Easter and Semana Santa.

Chapter 59 – Family Ties

The family arrived at Casa Miramar to a cooler full of cold beer and steaks on the grill. It was a long day, with a flight from Kentucky and then a five-hour drive from Tucson. My grandson Zachary had his first dip in the pool and he loved it. It was a chilly evening but it didn't bother him. He stayed in the water until it was time for bed. Everyone is tired and happy to be in Mexico.

The Mexican Easter Bunny left Zachary a chocolate bunny along with lots of other chocolate. I went to the Mercado and purchased tons of yummy pastries for everyone. You could say I am eating vicariously through my family. I have eyed the pastries for three months now and have never had one, but am told they are as delicious as they look. Watching others eat them is almost as good as doing it myself and it's much less fattening. Am I obsessed?

The day was spent lounging around the pool and catching up on family news. Zachary and I took the dogs for a walk on the beach, and then I went for my morning run. The tide was out and the sand was hard, making it a bit easier. I'm getting closer to that endorphin high—I can feel it!

Easter afternoon was a sightseeing tour of San Carlos and

a visit to Jon Jens Charters to return the new cooler that Mike purchased in return for the smaller one he took home full of yellowfin. Jon told us that he found a filet in his freezer that was suppose to go to Mike, so if we wanted it, he would bring it in on Monday and we could pick it up. Fresh fish—without having to actually go fishing? Of course we'll take it! A big thanks to Mike for that one! Zach bonded with Luke Boy just as I did. He loves dogs almost as much as me.

We spent some time on the beach at the Soggy Peso where we also had a snack. Chad was not impressed with the crab tostada like all my friends seem to be. I haven't tried it because it's not on my diet, but Chad said it was too fishy for his palate. I guess when you're raised on King crab, any other crab can't possibly compare. The kite-boarders were amazing—that's a water sport that looks like fun. However, when you crash the kite into the surf, it's hell getting it back up in the air.

The night is early on Easter Sunday and we feed the dogs and kitties, who are all waiting patiently when we arrive home. Zachary took another dip in the pool (the kid had to be a fish in a prior life!) and at 9 we gave it up. It seems the sun, sand and relaxation makes sleep come early at Casa Miramar.

Chapter 60 – Nose Piercings

The day started off with a walk on the beach with Zach and the dogs. He is so good with Zippy and she is glad he is around. Walking with OgDog is pretty slow, so running with Zach makes her much happier! She used to drag him around with the leash but he is now big enough to drag her around. I did my usual beach run afterwards with lots of sweating! The sun has definitely gotten hotter.

Off to diet center for my weekly weigh-in only to find them closed. Last week was Holy Week and apparently this week is Resurrection Week, so many businesses are closed for a few more days. It looks like I will have to wait until Wednesday to find out if I lost more kilos.

Later in the morning we went to the shell beach and oyster factory. Zachary found lots of shells to take home and I found fish and bird bones. The factory had interesting jewelry made from the pearls and we read about the history of pearl farming. By this time it is really hot, so the pool is sounding really good. Back to the casa for an afternoon spent in recliners watching Zachary swim while we read. I told him he would look like a prune if he didn't get out of the water soon. It would be nice to have that kind of energy—non-stop swimming for about three hours.

Jeremy and Chad went to explore San Carlos, and when they didn't return by 4 p.m., Natasha, Zach, Debbie and I decided on a trip to Guaymas. Debbie said she had wanted to get her nose pierced but everyone gave her such a hard time about it in West Virginia that she still hadn't done it. Well, I know just the place. Sergio, here we come! But when we get to his office, it too is closed. By this time we are starving, so I take them to one of my favorite restaurants for dinner, Poncho Villa. Zachary and his Nana order virgin piña coladas. Dinner was delicious, as usual. On the way home we again swing by the piercing doctor's office and find him there. I guess another piercing is meant to be.

Zachary thinks we are crazy and gets a big belly laugh out the idea of us getting our noses pierced. It was funny hearing him laugh so hard and we were all cracking up. He will remember his silly Mema and Nana doing this for years to come. And we did it! Both of us walked out with jewels on the left side of our noses. Plus I got two extra holes in my ears, just in case I want more earrings in them.

Back to the casa we find the guys waiting on us. Oh well, you snooze, you lose—we didn't wait around for your sorry butts. Apparently, they got sidetracked at Froggies and ended up being gone for seven hours. Sorry you guys missed out on all our fun.

Early tomorrow morning we have made plans with Antonio to hike Mt.Teta Kawi. It's the mountain I missed because I got sick the first time, and the second time I made excuses about packing for Austin. Third time is the charm, so my butt will be going up that bad boy tomorrow, one way or another. Stay tuned . . .

Chapter 61 – Mt. Teta Kawi

OMG, now that was extreme rock climbing. I am so glad I decided NOT to run on the beach first; otherwise, I would probably still be on that mountain. At times we were actually crawling up rocks, finding toeholds wherever we could. But that's not the worst part; coming down in loose gravel was extremely tenuous. I didn't get pictures of the actual hike because Antonio had to carry my camera in his pack while I struggled to get my body up and then down the mountain. Speaking of Antonio, he scaled it without a hitch. This is a hike he knows well and ends up helping all hikers in his care achieve their goal of reaching the summit.

What a quest. My first mistake was eating cereal on the way there. At one point I had to stop because I was sure it was coming back up. After a short breather and a drink of water, I was fine except for shaky legs and a shortness of breath. Okay, enough whining. We DID IT! The view from the top was unbelievable, which made it totally worth the challenge. We were very glad to get back to the car—on the mountain it looked like a toy. Antonio didn't even break a sweat, and had the nerve to suggest we run to San Carlos when we got down. Silly man!

The hike took us about three hours total—not bad for beginners. Natasha was sure she would not make it down; it's the height thing and the loose gravel that made her wonder. But with Antonio's help, she did fine. We all wondered about Chad—all those cervezas at Froggies yesterday made his ascent questionable. But he persevered! We had made the decision earlier not to bring Zachary or Jeremy along and it's a good thing. It would not have been fun for either of them.

Did we have fun? At times I wonder, but overall, yes. It's a great feeling to have done it. Will I do it again? That's questionable, at best. My legs are going to tell me all about it tomorrow. We crawled back to the pool and collapsed for the rest of the afternoon. Zachary was back in the pool, swimming and having a grand time. At sunset we went to the La Playa de Cortes Hotel on the beach for sunset. Although it's a short hike from the casa, we elected to take the car. Zachary met an Indian woodcarver and bought a sailfish. Piña coladas were not good at all, but the sunset was great. It's an early night for most of us; the mountain hike is still with us. Tomorrow, Chad and I will golf at the country club in San Carlos—that is, if we can still walk!

Chapter 62 – The Final Weigh-In

The legs are extremely sore today and not moving well, particularly on anything downhill, especially steps. I tried running but gave it up—too painful! For whatever reason, I am sorer than Chad and Tash and the second day is supposed to be even worst. Aye yi yi!

But the good news today? I did my final weigh-in at the diet center and lost one more kilo. The diet doctor told me I had reached my ideal weight and should not lose more than four more kilos to stay in the correct range for my body type. That makes me so happy! It worked and I feel great. Instead of the usual acupressure jolt, she taped a tiny metal ball (grain-of-rice size) to my jaw and shoulder points and gave me a maintenance diet for the road. I have totally changed my attitude about food.

After weigh-in, we went to the Wednesday market to browse. I had already made up my mind that there would be no more treasures for me. I can barely fit all my things in VeVe as it is, plus I have tons of stuff in Vashon to pick up. The market seemed much smaller this week, maybe because it is Resurrection Week. The only thing purchased in our group was food—carrot cake, and Zachary had something resembling a strawberry Popsicle.

Chad and I did manage to play nine holes of golf—first time for a desert course. It's different. The ball does not stick when it hits the green, but takes off on a roll. That can be good or bad, depending on the shot. The pro shop only charged us green fees and threw in free rental clubs for me. The guy said, *"Be happy and have fun."* We had a few good shots and many bad ones, but lots of laughs—and that's what it's all about. Serious golfing? I don't think so.

We were meeting the rest of our crew at Froggies for hamburgers at 6. After golf we have an hour to kill, so headed to the health club for a much-needed Jacuzzi. Wow, did it feel good! We were surprised when we arrived at Froggies that Zachary could not come in, not even to eat. I guess it's more of a drinking establishment than a restaurant. So, I suggested Los Barcos in Guaymas. The fountain runs every day from 7-7:30 and we timed it right. The music and the colored-water streams welcomed us downtown, where we had a good dinner and then called it a night.

The following morning the legs were still really sore and not willing to run the beach. We invited Antonio to bring his girls over for a swim with Zachary while we went for some pampering. Debbie and I scheduled a facial and some waxing, and Natasha had her eyebrows done. She ended up waiting on us for over two hours because that's how long the facial lasted. It was extremely relaxing.

We were going to cook on the grill for our last night, but changed our minds and went to Poncho Villa instead. Who wants to cook? There just happened to be a festival in the square across the street from the restaurant. Zachary found a wooden train and some delicious ice cream—he didn't get the tequila flavor, but opted for, guess what? Piña colada. Debbie has been looking everywhere for some mescal to take home for Mike. In all the times I've been to Mexico I have never seen tequila with a worm in the bottom—not that I have ever looked. But at the festival, there it was big as life. One more thing to cross off the list as time is getting short in Guaymas. We leave tomorrow morning for Tucson. Today marks the end of our Mexican vacation. Little did I know how true that statement would later become.

Part V

Stranded in Old Mexico

"Not all those who wander are lost"
—J. R. R. Tolkien

Chapter 63 – Dog Smuggling 101

Friday morning we are ready to leave for Tucson at 10. The hardest thing was saying goodbye to Antonio. I am grateful for the patience and encouragement he gave me to keep pushing myself to run, and showing me how to breathe properly so I wouldn't give up. Thanks, Antonio. Just know you have a friend in Alaska whenever you want to hold boot camp in Homer! The dogs and I will miss you, especially Zippy!

We said our goodbyes and got on the road. Zachary and the four dogs were with me; and Chad, Tash, Debbie and Jeremy followed in the other car. Everyone else is flying out of Tucson tomorrow morning, but we still have tonight to hang out. Zach and I decide on Motel 6 for our destination. The dogs are welcome and they have a pool so we can go swimming when we get there.

We passed through Hermosillo, the largest city in Sonora (800,000 people) and also the capital of the state. It took awhile to get through the traffic and somehow our cars got separated, but no worries. We'll hook up on the other side. Zach and I went through the first tollbooth out of the city, assuming everyone was ahead of us. A few miles past the toll, I heard several beeps and noticed the dashboard gauge blinking red. Oh NO! Not again—the temperature light! This is déjà vu, just like when I left for Austin, but now I have Zachary with me! It seems Mexico has a grip on me that won't let go.

Of course we pull over immediately and shut the engine off. I realize my cell phone is not working and I have no way to call the other car. How long will it take them to notice we are missing? What are we going to do? Seven- year-old Zachary appears very calm as we sit there and talk about our situation. The dogs are hot, we're hot, it's too far to walk, and we have no phone service. We wait for a bit, then try moving forward again, but almost immediately the red light beeps on. This isn't going to work. VeVe is REALLY hot!

About 15 minutes later, Natasha pulls in back of VeVe. They had stopped for a burrito and were actually behind and not ahead of us, thank goodness. I explain the situation and Nana Debbie comes over to see if Zach is okay and when he saw her he burst into tears, sobbing, *"We're never going to get home!"*

After assessing the situation, Chad remembered a sign a few miles back that said Mercedes Service. Tash did a U-turn in the car and headed back to get help while Jeremy and I waited with VeVe. A short while later they returned followed by a truck and two Mexicans that spoke NO English—nada. Apparently, Chad had to wake one guy up. He was taking a siesta in his truck and not particularly happy about the interruption—but for 30 pesos he finally agreed to come have a look. Picture this: five of us on the side of the freeway in 80-degree weather with our Spanish dictionary trying to communicate with two Mexican guys, who incidentally looked like Cheech & Chong. Hilarious, if we could only laugh.

The guys continued talking in very fast Spanish, even after we told them "non español." They were pointing under the hood, pulling out fuses, putting water in the reservoir, and crawling under the car. I was desperately trying to make them understand that all I needed was a tow to Nogales—a three-hour drive from here—telling them I would pay them well to get me there. They continued shaking their heads. No way, no can do.

The bottom line: They have no way of fixing my car here, and they can't pull me with their truck because I have front-wheel-drive. I need a flatbed truck. Getting that point across was extremely difficult until Tash actually DREW a picture of a flatbed truck on a napkin. Ah, now they get it! They were finished with us and just wanted to get their money and leave.

After all, it is siesta time.

We wanted them to get us a flatbed truck before leaving, but we can't understand what they are saying. Finally, Chad gets in their truck and they are turning back toward Hermosillo. Well, maybe someone should follow? Tash does another U-turn. While Jeremy and I stay with VeVe everyone else races after Cheech & Chong, who have taken Chad back to the service station to call the police, who in turn are going to get a tow truck to come get us. Whew! Maybe some help soon?

Chad paid the guys for trying to help, said goodbye, muchas gracias, and everyone returned to VeVe to wait for the tow. In the meantime, I flagged down a truck pulling a trailer as a second option. Of course, it's the language thing again, but basically the driver told me he had no way to get my car onto his trailer. At this point I could almost lift VeVe onto the truck myself! Muchas gracias, señor. Thanks for stopping anyhow.

It seemed like forever until we saw a flatbed heading our way. When the driver got out, I asked him to tow me to Nogales, and in limited English he said *"No, but the tow is free to Hermosillo."* Okay, so Hermosillo it is! He loads VeVe onto the truck, with the dogs and I inside. Wow! What a bird's-eye view from up here! This would be so totally illegal in the States, but is merely another adventure in Mexico! I wave goodbye to my family and assure them I will call as soon as I get to Tucson later tonight.

We're actually enjoying the ride on the flatbed. The tow truck arrives at the tollbooth and I am required to pay again. Didn't I just do this a couple hours ago? Oh well, I pay as the driver starts unloading me at the gate. Wait a minute; I thought you were taking me to a mechanic? He said that a mechanic is on his way to pick me up here. I understand, but don't you dare leave me until the mechanic gets here, Ok? He smiles and nods at me, pointing to yet another flatbed truck coming toward us. And this mechanic speaks some English. I'm feeling a little better now. He said we are going another 10 miles, so he loads us onto his truck to go wherever it is he's taking us—presumably a garage.

Sure enough, we pull into a place called Santa Cruz Workshop, apparently owned by the driver, Alejandro, and his brother, Alfredo. He unloads us, hands me a business card and pulls VeVe into a shady stall, where his mechanic is waiting. The dogs and I will just sit in the car since we have no place else to go. It's only 2 p.m. so we might still make Tucson today. . . in my dreams.

They have to troubleshoot the problem and start by replacing the thermostat. AGAIN? Remember that was done last time. Well okay, but it didn't work this time. Next they change a censor. Nope, that didn't do it either. My hopes of making Tucson tonight are fading as the hours pass with each negative test. Looks like this may take longer than I expected, so I need to come up with Plan B, spending the night here.

I left the dogs in the car and walked to the nice hotel

across the street to see about a room. The price was right at $45/night, but there was a small problem. The desk clerk said no pets allowed. Okay, moving on to the motel a few doors down - not nearly as nice, a cheaper rate, but no pets allowed here either. In fact, there is a major cultural difference. No pets are allowed in ANY of the hotels! Yikes, now what?

By 7 p.m. the car is still overheating and they are calling it a night—closing time is normally 6. Apparently, there might be a problem with the water pump (now I'm seeing $$'s) and they can't get one from the dealer until tomorrow. Alejandro said he prefers getting the part from VW, and not Auto Zone—that's a good sign. BTW, VeVe was built here in Mexico so it's good she's being repaired here!

I explained my hotel problem to Alejandro and told him I would sneak my dogs into the room but I needed my car to do so. He volunteered his car and said he would help me. Great! I ran back across the street to rent the room; hopefully they won't remember anything about the dogs I mentioned earlier. No problem. I get the key to room 113 and race back to the garage and load the dogs and our necessities into his car. We drive past the desk, park in front of my room door and quietly carry the dogs in, one by one, under a blanket, Zippy weighing a

TON. Okay, we're now safe for the night. Good deal. See you guys in the morning after you get the water pump. We said goodnight and I shut the door, or at least thought I did.

The next thing I see is Zippy standing at the door with her nose peering out the crack and her tail wagging wildly. Oh NOOOO! Busted already? I run to the door and see that room service is delivering dinner next door. The girl is smiling at Zippy as I yank her back inside. I put my finger to my mouth, giving her the hush sign, and she nods. That was a close one, DoDog! Hopefully our secret is safe. Otherwise? I'm not going there.

We're exhausted. I need a drink. Good thing I brought the rum for Cuba Libres! I went to the bar and got the required Coca Light and limes. Once we got settled into the room and had some dinner, we went straight to sleep—dreaming of a new water pump and getting back on the road first thing in the morning. What a day for a Silly Woman with four dogs and a broken-down VW Beetle called VeVe!

Chapter 64 – Dog Smuggling Continues. . .

Saturday morning we're up early, packed and ready to go. I decide to run across the street to see how the pump installation is coming along. The mechanic is working on getting the old one out and thinks we should be on our way around 2, if everything goes as planned. Great! Just a minor setback, but we are ready to move on.

Since checkout time is not until 1 p.m. at the hotel, we are going to stay there for the morning. It's much cooler in the air-conditioned room than sitting in VeVe. I mosey back from the garage and nearly panic when I see what appears to be two hotel managers knocking on my door, with their keys out, ready to open it up. I yell, *"un momento, por favor,"* running over to them—thinking now I've had it!

"No pets allowed" is all I could make out. Okay, I said, we're leaving anyway—no point in trying to talk my way out of this; they seem to know the dogs are in there. They smile and continue their rounds as I collapse inside the room, wondering how they could possibly know. I didn't hear any barking when I got to the door and the Do Not Disturb sign was still posted on the outside. In fact, the dogs are still asleep on the bed. Someone from the day shift must have remembered me from

yesterday. No worries. Alejandro is picking us up at 12:45 and it's 11 now. We'll just relax here until then.

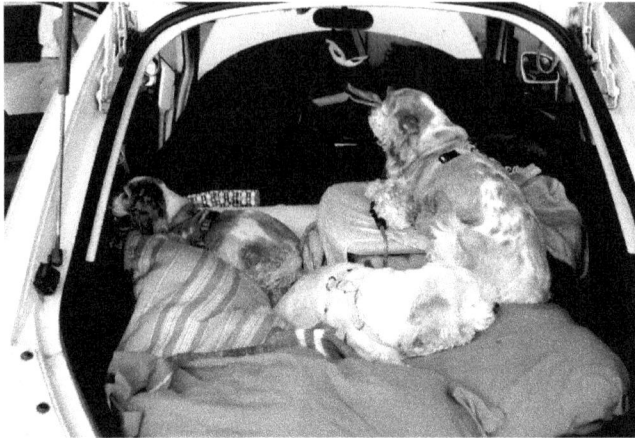

Alejandro shows up and has news, but it's not great. The new water pump is in, but it did not fix the problem, even though there was a broken part inside it. VeVe is still overheating, so more troubleshooting is required. We check out of the room and return to the garage. I unload the dogs into my car, leaving both doors open, along with the back boot door, so the air can circulate inside. It's already caliente. I assume my position in the driver's seat to be available for starting and stopping the engine, as requested. I spend the rest of the time reading a Frances Mayes' book about traveling around the world for a year, just to get my mind off the situation at hand.

We are obviously not getting out of here by 2, and if we

don't make it by 4, we will be here another night – I won't drive to a border town after dark! I suppose sleeping in the car tonight is a thought? A short-lived one at that—no way! Aye yi yi! Four o'clock comes and goes, and I have a mini-meltdown with Alfredo, the other brother. He ASSURES me that they will get it fixed, but it's going to take more time to diagnose the problem, something I'm short on at the moment. Okay, so I need to back up, breathe deeply through my nose, and meditate. Everything happens for a reason, right? Patience is a virtue, think positive, and so on and so forth. The deep breathing actually does help me relax and get back to my book.

I notice that the spaniels are sleeping well in the backseat, but what about Zippy? She is nowhere to be found. Oh no, apparently she got bored and jumped out the back without me even knowing. A basset hound loose on the streets of Hermosillo? Great. Now I have another problem. I rush out to the street, calling her, looking both ways. Where did she go and how long has she been gone, I wonder. I see Alfredo walking between the other cars in the garage, slightly bent over. I call out and ask if he's seen my dog, and he smiles. He is bent over because he is dragging her by the collar back to the car. She didn't go far—just down to the office to see the guys.

215

She knew I wasn't happy with her when I told her, 'Up front with me, girly, so I can keep an eye on you!' With her head and ears nearly dragging the floor, she got in, circled the seat a few times and fell right back to sleep. Can't fault the girl for wanting some entertainment. We're all pretty tired of our situation about now.

It's now 6:30 p.m. and the mechanic has been working non-stop since 8 a.m.—I didn't even see him take a lunch break. He is mumbling to himself a bit and then he starts tossing tools around – not really throwing them, but obviously upset. Now he's having a meltdown! Oh brother! Since he doesn't speak English, I call Alfredo over to lighten up the situation. They speak in Spanish and then Alfredo turns to translate for me. Okay, tomorrow is Sunday, he said, and the garage is closed. However, the mechanic has agreed to come in and pull the radiator in VeVe first thing in the morning—but he desperately needs a break right now. That's cool, I totally understand, and it IS Saturday night in the city. We all need a break right now!

Apparently, pulling the radiator is a huge job—about six hours to get it out because much of the front end has to be disassembled. For some reason the water is not circulating at the bottom and the only way to find out why is to pull it completely out of the car. At this point I either trust them or I don't, and I really do believe they are doing everything they can to get me back on the road. So I say okay, this sounds like a plan to me.

OMG, will we ever get out of Mexico or will I have to first get a job to pay for this repair? This is going to cost a fortune, but at this point I don't have another choice. I'm thinking a minimum of 10,000 pesos—roughly $800—and feeling like that's only if I'm lucky. The labor alone is already 20-plus hours and we still have tomorrow and all the parts to consider! Enough! I quickly make up my mind to forget about the cost. I just want to be mobile again. I'll think about the money when I get the bill.

I ran across the street to the hotel, hoping I could check in with the night shift again. No problem; they offer me the same room, number 113. At least that's good news. No one says a word about the incident this morning, or asks about the perros. Again we load the dogs in Alejandro's car and sneak them in the room. I have already decided that once we get inside, I am staying put for the night. I definitely don't want to risk getting caught again. We're exhausted—something about being in the heat all afternoon really makes us tired. I make myself a drink, feed the dogs and order chicken from the restaurant that I will personally pick up when ready. No room service for room 113!

At some point I have to start thinking about what happens IF VeVe cannot be repaired. What will I do? I email a friend that has a car for sale in Seattle—that might be an option if I need another car to get us back to Alaska. Now I feel guilty. Poor VeVe. I can't believe I'm even thinking she might not make it.

Since hotels are so un-dog friendly here in Mexico, I'm sure a bus ride with dogs is out of the question, so I need to line up a rescue operation. I email my friend in Austin to see if she would come get us if it comes to that—maybe with a trailer to pull VeVe back to the U.S.? I then send out a lifeline to Juanita in Vashon to see if she has ANY friends in Hermosillo that can help us out, or suggestions for our predicament. Juanita ALWAYS has answers.

I feel much better being pro-active in the event the situation doesn't get resolved soon. But for tonight we are safe and sound in the NO-DOG Premier Hotel, where four perros are softly snoring underneath the covers in room 113

Chapter 65 - Evicted for Smuggling Perros, NOT!

Good morning, Hermosillo! It's Sunday and sunny in Sonora, Mexico—another day in paradise. Maybe if I was still at the casita in Guaymas, but stranded in paradise? That's a different story. Since the mechanic had a major meltdown last night, I have decided to give him some space this morning— resisting my urge to hover over his shoulder like the anxious American that I am at the moment. The dogs and I are going to hang out in the hotel room until noon, and then I will check in at the garage.

We are having a leisurely morning until I turn on the TV and see Dr. Phil on Mexican TV telling the world how to apply common sense to daily life. Duh! Can you believe it? And he makes millions doing this. Needless to say, the TV didn't stay on long—I can't bear to watch crap. Instead, I turned on my Mac Book to check email—at least that makes me feel somewhat connected while I'm stuck south of the border.

So the good news: the Toyota Camry in Seattle IS available and in my price range if I need to get another vehicle to get us back to Alaska, and a rescue operation is also confirmed if I need one, as long as no ransom is required. Now what does that mean? Juanita emailed me with lots of ideas, such as: call

Antonio and have him call Francisco (our Spanish tutor) and have him call the garage and translate for you. Call Tammie in San Carlos (an American realtor friend) to see if she has contacts in Hermosillo, and her boyfriend is Mexican and could also call the garage and translate for you. Juanita's final words were: I know it's scary right now, but you'll be okay. I know that to be true.

It's about 11:30 a.m. and I can't bear to wait any longer. I have to check on VeVe, so I get dressed and run across the street to the garage. Imagine my surprise when I see the large metal gates closed and the place totally locked up. Maybe he's working behind the locked entrance since the garage is technically closed on Sunday. I bang on the gate and say hola—no response. What the hell? Checkout at the hotel is less than an hour, so I have to figure this out FAST.

I'm back to the room in a flash (fortunately, management is not hanging out at my door), frantically looking for the Santa Cruz Workshop business card that I finally find in the back pocket of my jean shorts. After three attempts to call the number and the access code not working, I ring the front desk and ask them to dial it for me. They called me back and said there was no answer. I look at the card again and see a cell number at the bottom, so I call the front desk back and ask them to try a second number for me. She rings back to say she will connect me, and then the phone goes dead. Another ring and I have Alejandro on the line.

"*Where is the mechanic, the garage is locked, I have to check out, the dog food is locked in the car, your mechanic was supposed to pull the radiator this morning, when WILL VeVe be fixed?*" And on and on I go. He quietly said, "*I don't understand.*" His English is really good, but now it's me that's talking really fast and he's having a hard time keeping up with me. I'M having a hard time keeping up with me. So, I shut up so he can speak.

Apparently, the mechanic worked all morning and got the radiator out, and will work on it first thing tomorrow morning (Monday). But I don't understand, I tell him; I thought he was going to work on it today. We go back and forth, getting nowhere. He tells me that he is headed to the garage to actually have a look at the radiator, so I ask him to stop by my room (he knows where it is) to let me know what he finds, and to explain to me what's happening. He agreed and said he would be here in about an hour. In the meantime, I obviously need to rent room 113 for yet another night. GAWD, will it ever end?

Back to the front desk—keep in mind it is now the day shift that I am dealing with, the ones who busted me two days ago. They take my money for one more night and I return to the room to wait on Alejandro. My phone rings and I think it's him calling back, but instead it's the clerk at the front desk. Sorry, she says, but NO DOGS are allowed at the hotel; you must put them in your car. IN MY CAR? If only I had one. I tell her that is not possible because the car is locked in the garage across the street. She then tells me her manager said I would have to leave. LEAVE, I have nowhere to go! She said she understood and would speak to her manager to see if he would make an excepción because of the circumstances. He'd better because I have already decided I am NOT leaving. Now I'm pissed, and where the hell IS Alejandro? It's been way over an hour.

I stand guard at the front door, all the while looking out the window. I don't want any surprise visits from management. I tried calling Alejandro on his cell again—NO answer. Woody keeps going to the door and looking at me. I tried to explain to him that it is okay to pee in the bathroom, but he doesn't get it because he is trained to pee outside. Finally, the desk clerk calls back to apologize, saying she understands my situation but the manager won't budge. I have to leave. I thank her for trying and tell her I will be right there and I want to speak to the manager! It's good that this is out in the open now because I am staying, one way or the other. I am so tired of worrying about getting evicted!

Back to the front desk and ready to get this over with once and for all. I am asked to wait un momento as the clerk disappears into the office and an older Mexican gentleman comes out to meet me, not looking too happy at all. I immediately start blabbing about why I have to stay at the hotel with my dogs for one more night and that I will gladly pay more pesos. He shakes his head no and points to the sign, NO PETS. I just keep talking about being homeless with nowhere to go, having the dogs in the heat, not speaking the language, being scared, etc. I explain about the car and how the garage is locked after they promised to work on my car today, and tell him it will be ready tomorrow, blah, blah, blah. His response was *"what if it's NOT ready tomorrow? What will you do then?"* (good question). But, I assure him it WILL be ready tomorrow (or I'm going to kick some serious ass).

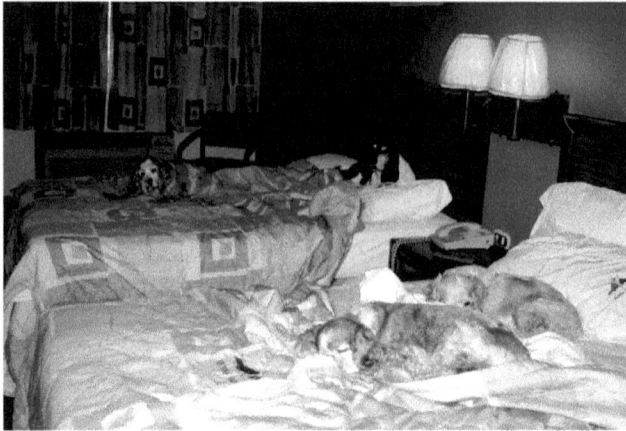

How about if I keep the dogs locked in the bathroom? (Fat chance). Ahhh, but I could tell he liked that idea, so I continue to elaborate on how they would remain locked up until we check out. Now I am getting somewhere. He finally relented and made an excepción for just una más noche. "And the dogs will stay in the bathroom?" he said again. "Si, señor, of course they will." Wheew! Glad that is finally over! Woody, I can take you out to pee at last!

I didn't have to shed a tear but I was ready to as a last-ditch effort before totally going off on him if it had come to that. Fortunately, it did not. Otherwise, I would probably be in a Mexican jail right now, and four perros would be in the animal shelter wondering what happened to the air-conditioned room with the comfy bed.

Since the cat is out of the bag with management or, in this

case, the dog, we can now go for a much-needed walk. All four perros are ecstatic to get out of the room to relieve themselves. We stroll right past the front desk and onto the street. Woody is so happy that he pees on every bush we pass. And, still no Alejanedro. Where the hell is he and why won't he answer his cell phone? Is he really going to be a no-show? I trusted these guys and now I'm not sure what to think.

I wait awhile longer and finally walk to the grocery store to pick up some dog food. After feeding the dogs, I settle in for the night. I should have something to eat, but I'm really not the least bit hungry. Tucson is only three hours from here, but without transportation in the desert, that's a long way. I can only hope that VeVe gets on the road tomorrow. Otherwise??? I will call the Austin rescue.

I've been reading a book, "The Instruction," how to live the life your soul intended, written by Scottish psychic Ainslie MacLeod, who lives on Vashon Island. Ainslie talks about having spirit guides that can help us through life if we ask them for guidance. I'm sitting on the hotel bed and decide, why not? I'm in a situation out of my control right now and I could use some help. I close my eyes, breathe deeply and ask my spirit guides for their help in getting VeVe back on the road.

It's 9 p.m., and we've had another exhausting day. The phone rings and I freeze—not the front desk again?

"Hola," I say into the receiver and hear a man's voice. *"Hello, who is this? Alejandro, is that you? Where were you? I thought you were coming by today? What about my car?"* Okay, so I'm doing it again. Shut up and let him talk.

He's asking me if I want him to stop by tonight or in the morning.

"Tonight, right now, by all means. Gracias, señor."

I throw some clothes on, get my hotel key and wait outside my door for him. I see him walking across the parking lot and run to meet him.

"Buenas noches, señor." He then said the most amazing thing.

"Do you want your car tonight or tomorrow morning?"

"What? It's ready?"

"Si."

"It's repaired and ready to go?"

"Si"

"What happened? I thought you said it would be tomorrow before the mechanic looked at it. This is great! What was wrong with it?" Again, I'm blabbing out of control and

226

Alejandro is looking confused. I need to shut up and let him speak.

Apparently, after talking with me earlier today, he called the mechanic at home and explained my situation with the dogs and the need for me to get on the road quickly. They both have been at the garage all afternoon, working on the radiator, getting the main hose unclogged—apparently caused by water sediment from overheating. Doing mucho troubleshooting to be sure the problem was fixed, and I was good to go, before contacting me. OMG, I am so happy and stunned. We walk back to the garage where the mechanic has the car running and ready for me to test. VeVe looks happy and sounds great. And the best news: The temperature gauge is where it should be. I don't really understand what clogged the radiator hose other than sediment, but do I care? NOT, as long as it's fixed! Again, the Mexican people have gone out of their way for me.

Okay, so do I want to take the car tonight or pick it up in the morning? Oh tonight, by all means! They don't take credit cards because the machine is down, so I need an ATM. Alejandro offers to take me to the bank tonight. He hands me the invoice and, although it's in Spanish, I can read the bottom-line figure of 3,975 pesos. Only 3,975? That's it? I do a quick calculation in my head and realize that's only about $350, a third of what I expected. It actually turned out to be $304 for about 32 hours of straight labor, a new water pump, censor, and a thermostat. Again, I am stunned. So stunned that I just get enough pesos at the bank to pay the bill and on the way back to the garage realize I need to give the mechanic a much-deserved tip. I'll definitely do that before I leave mañana. Sometimes I forget how much the Mexican people rely on American tips. And these guys definitely deserve one.

I pull VeVe in front of room 113; order a rib-eye steak from the restaurant (the appetite is back), and fall asleep, knowing our time in Mexico is indeed short now—another chapter is slowly closing. We'll be on our way to Tucson in the morning and will officially check out of room 113 once and for all! Muchas gracias to the hotel management for understanding our predicament and making a much-needed excepción for us, and a special muchas gracias to Santa Cruz Workshop for working non-stop to get VeVe back on the road. We can't thank you enough! Mexican culture and the people are totalmente impresionante!

Part VI

On the Road Again

"I am not the same having seen the moon shine on the other side of the world"
—Mary Anne Radmache

Chapter 66 – Goodbye Beautiful Mexico

Good morning, Hermosillo! TODAY is indeed a beautiful day in paradise. We are so happy to be on the road early this morning—it's Monday! First, to the ATM to get the pesos for the mechanic's tip. Funny, when I pull in to the garage, Alfredo runs over and I tell him I want to see the mechanic. He says, *"What's the problem?"* I'm sure he's thinking something is wrong with my car again, and wondering if he will ever be rid of me! *"No problem, I just want to give him some extra pesos for the good job he did on my car,"* I said. He calls the mechanic over to where we are and I give him the traditionally Mexican greeting of a hug and kiss on the cheek as I put some pesos into his hand. He responds with a muchas gracias, señorita—big smile. I get back in VeVe, start her up and wave hasta luego, señor, and muchas, muchas gracias to you, too!

We are on the road again, as Willie Nelson would say. After about 15 minutes the dogs settle into the usual routine of VeVe cruising at 70 mph, the sun shining through the windows and the wind blowing over them; they will sleep until the car stops. The uneventful drive (as in NO flashing red lights) to Tucson is approximately 3.5 hours, and the line at the border is short—probably because it is Monday. We pass through customs in less than 10 minutes and are finally back on U.S. soil. Tucson feels very hot, dry and dusty as we head west on 1-10 toward Phoenix. The closer we get to Phoenix, the greener the landscape becomes. Did I mention that it feels so good to be on the road that we just keep going, stopping only occasionally for gas and a quick pee? After approximately 10 hours of driving, I decide that Motel 6 in Flagstaff is our destination for tonight. But first we are taking a small side trip through the back roads to Sedona. The red rocks are breathtaking and I make a mental note that this is definitely a place I want to return to explore and hike. I contact a friend living here, but she is tied up for the evening and suggested I stay over another day so we can get together tomorrow afternoon. I am ready to keep moving toward the Pacific Northwest mañana, so we'll have to catch up later. The road is calling.

We find our Motel 6 in Flagstaff and settle in early—from Hermosillo to Flagstaff in one day, crossing not only international borders but also many cultural borders along the way. Much to process in only a 12-hour period—that feels more like days than hours. I email another friend that is also living in Sedona to see if coffee is a possibility in the morning. Unfortunately, she is on her way to the Phoenix airport so that too, will have to wait until next time around. After a much needed rest, we are up at 5:30 a.m. and on the road by 8. The road winds us into Utah; Kanab, Zion National Park, Bryce Canyon and the eastern rim of the Grand Canyon. The scenery is spectacular on Route 89 and, even though it takes more time, it is well worth it. I have traveled across the U.S. many times but this is my first time on Route 89, and I am enjoying every minute of it. There is something very powerful about the terrain, a mystical sort of energy that emanates from the red rocks and draws me in.

OgDog is having an uncomfortable day—he is panting and can't seem to get settled in his seat. I finally pull over, get the Medicam out of the suitcase and give him a dose. It's an anti-inflammatory, pain medication that I don't use often, only when he seems to have discomfort. I move him to the back area on the doggie bed and invite Luce and Zippy to share the front seat with me, giving OgDog more room to stretch out in the back with Woody. It took about 30 minutes for the meds to kick in and then he was sleeping like a baby.

We have a very long day driving, approximately 650 miles total, crossing through Utah and into Idaho. Where is the Motel 6 that welcomes all dogs when I need it? I know, at least 100 miles back. I waited too long to stop, I'm really tired, it's late and we're in the middle of nowhere right now, so I pulled into an alternative motel. The owner asked me if I had any dogs and I said no before I even realized it—a flashback from Hermosillo. After filling out the paperwork, I looked at her and said: *"I cannot tell a lie, I do have dogs."* Well, she wanted $10/dog, with a two-dog minimum. OMG! I'm thinking what difference does it make if it's two or four dogs? You either allow them or you don't. I could probably get away with the four dogs, but after my latest adventure, I don't even want to go there. Moving on. . .

I told her to cancel the request—that I would continue another 50 miles to Twin Falls, Idaho, where there has to be a Motel 6. Another 30 minutes on the road and at last we see the familiar red and blue sign. I knew there had to be one soon. It's after 10 p.m. when we get settled into our room, and it feels so good to get out of the car and stretch out. The dogs have a quick dinner, jump on the bed and go straight to sleep. I had a shower and was close behind them.

I realize Casa Miramar and Guaymas are becoming distant memories already, so much has happened in such a short period of time. We are closer home than I imagined in only two days. If we get a good start tomorrow, we could actually be in Seattle tomorrow night. Now that's a concept.

Chapter 67 – The Beautiful Pacific Northwest

We made it! There were times at the Premier Hotel in Hermosillo that I wondered if we would ever get out of Mexico and to the Pacific Northwest. Now that experience seems ages ago. We got a 9 a.m. start Wednesday from Twin Falls and actually gained an hour on Pacific time, arriving in Woodinville at 7:30. We are staying with Sharon and Mike for a couple weeks before continuing on to Alaska. Over the years we have become regulars here, so the dogs are very familiar with our "room" in Woodinville. In fact, when I turn onto Bear Creek Road, they become extremely animated in the backseat, knowing exactly where we are—dogs are amazing that way. By the time I reach the driveway, Zippy is actually standing with her front paw pressing into my left shoulder, barely able to contain herself. We are so happy to be here, even if it is freezing! Sharon and Mike are in Maui, so the temperature in the house is about 50. . . brrrr. My blood certainly thinned out in Mexico! Ahhh, to be in our familiar bed—it feels great under the down comforter. Life is good!

Thursday morning is gray and rainy—a great day to sleep in, since we have the house to ourselves! The dogs and I stay warm by cuddling in bed most of the day, catching up on emails, bills and writing chronicles. Later in the afternoon I make a trip to Safeway to get some food, and could not believe the prices compared to Guaymas. Sticker-shock overload! I bought some asparagus that was on sale for $4.99 a pound. Yikes!—in Mexico it was $1.25. The cost is substantially higher on everything, and will be even more in Homer. One could certainly get used to the Mexican prices for both food and drink. I see a few spots of sun on my way, but the air is definitely chilly. Guess it's good that we are doing the gradual trip back to Alaska, allowing ourselves time to get acclimated to the higher prices and cooler weather. The dogs are even shivering! Friday promises sunshine for my trip to Vashon Island to pick up les trés jours collected in Washington prior to heading south of the border.

It's amazing how many clothes I have accumulated in the short time of being here. It was so much fun foraging at the Goodwill in Seattle and Granny's Attic on Vashon. I spend the afternoon getting reacquainted with my treasures by trying everything on. All of this will be added to the full container of Mexican clothes from Wednesday markets. Yikes! Serious packing skills are required to fit everything in VeVe for the trip home.

It seems like an eternity since I lived on Vashon Island, a community that feels similar to Homer. Speaking of Homer. . . I am ready to be back home for the summer. And for the fall, where will I be? Hard to say. I have a few ideas. . . such as living large and having a birthday party—in PARIS. Everyone is invited!

Chapter 68 – Reviewing Intentions

The sun is finally out in the Seattle area and it's time to start running again. Since the breakdown in Hermosillo and the trip north, it's already been a week. I have obviously been slacking with the routine, so I thought it might be really hard to start up again. However, two things are different here: 1) I finally have the proper shoes and they are really light – the ones in Mexico were hiking tennies, and heavy! And: 2) I am running on pavement and not the soft sand on the beach. Later, when I clocked my distance, I was amazed that it was exactly two miles and I wasn't even breathing heavy! I really think the endorphins are kicking in too, because at one point I felt like I could just keep going.

I just reviewed the goals I set back in January for going to Mexico. Here's what I did and did not accomplish and how/why:

1. Exercising and eating organic. I think boot camp and running the beach definitely covers the exercise end of things. Plus, in Mexico it is easy to eat organic—lots of fresh fruits and vegetables and the meat is hormone-free.

2. Learning to speak some Spanish. My Spanish tutor, Francisco, would say I learned a few words and phrases, but need mucho más práctica. And, agreeing to do some homework

might have helped.

3.   Making pictures. I did do that—lots and lots of images.

4.   Reading many books by the pool. I did read a few books by the pool, but not many. Naps, drinking and pampering seemed to interfere with reading time. The "Zone of Tolerance" was a favorite, chronicling the red-light district of Guaymas back in the '70s.

5.   Teaching yoga. I did lead one practice for Maggie and me. And I did DO yoga a few times in between boot camps.

6.   Taking tennis lessons. Juanita and I bought racquets, does that count? And we went to the club and watched a lesson, how about that? There was never enough time in the day for tennis lessons. Sounds like a good reason to return, don't you think?

7.   Getting my bellybutton and ears pierced. Oh yes, we did do that. And the piercing doctor made sure it was painless. Plus, he was part Italian, handsome, and a flirt!

8.   Getting a tattoo. No time for this one. Maybe later.

9.   Getting my face waxed and my body massaged! Ahhh, the face waxing. Remember they even waxed my nose? - not my crotch, but my nose! No need for a body massage in

Mexico, I was limp as a noodle already.

10. Getting some metal taken out of my mouth. Nada—the closest thing I had was the teeth cleaning and the erotic cheek and lip massage. Remember the dentist in San Carlos? Aye yi yi!

11. Drinking many margaritas to ease all the pain! Not on the diet, but I did have my fair share of straight tequila, gin martinis, and Cuba Libres! Oh and also Pear Absolut, straight up.

Not bad for a Silly Woman.

Chapter 69 - Friends, Dogs & Art

So much fun seeing friends and hanging out in the Seattle area, here are just a few of the highlights:

Meeting Rich and Diana for lunch at Joey's in Bellevue. We ordered martinis (not as good as La Conquista), bellinis (really yummy but NOT on the diet) and chicken Caesar salads—hold the croutons, please. Over cocktails we decided another sailing trip with Captain Slime might be a fun vacation to plan. In the mid-'90s Rich and I were on a trip with the Captain in the Florida Keys—and other than constantly barking orders at me, it was a great time (apparently I was the first mate and didn't know it). We do love his sense of humor, and his sailing abilities rock! We definitely need to check with Slime to see if he's available and clarify that I am NOT the first mate this time. But I will volunteer to be bartender.

A trip to Marymoor Dog Park in Redmond with Gail and the dogs—over 40 acres where dogs run free with lots of trees to mark and butts to sniff. Water borders one side with designated areas for the so-inclined canine swimmers. It's a great place to catch up, get some exercise and hang out with frolicking dogs. My dogs truly enjoyed themselves, even OgDog who managed to keep up with the rest of the pack. I was so inspired watching the dogs interact that I am now photographing dog TAILS, a constantly moving target. Easier said than done, but it's a howl trying!

Hilltop House on First Hill. Gail teaches a weekly art class and invited me to be her assistant for the day. This retirement community is full of young, creative spirits, many in their 80s and 90s. I was particularly interested in Genoa, an artist who was a New York City fashion photographer in the '60s. She also worked for Magnum Photos and personally knew many of the great photojournalists of that era. The class today was touch drawing, a technique of applying paint to a surface, covering it with archival tissue paper, and then using the hands, fists, nails, etc., to press into the surface, creating various shapes and textures. We turned up the salsa music and people were on their feet swaying to the music and pressing into their paper. Once the drawing "feels" complete, the tissue is pulled off and placed face-up to dry. The drawings created were amazing—so much movement and feeling. It was so incredible to watch the creative process evolve, and Gail is a naturally gifted teacher. Thanks for sharing your experience with me.

A matinee with Robin, "State of Play," with Russell Crowe

and Ben Affleck. Robin made the trip to Woodinville this time; usually we meet on her turf in West Seattle. I suggested Red Robin's for a bite to eat after the flick—she flinched. What's wrong with Red Robin, anyhow? We just need a place to have a drink and some girl talk. Okay, so I agree—RR's certainly can't compare to one of her choices, Serious Pie—a Tom Douglas pizza joint in downtown Seattle. But it's not always all about the food, is it?

Picking up Sharon and Mike at SeaTac. Returning home from Maui, I volunteered to pick them up—Shar said bring whatever car you want. I picked her SUV because it is smaller and easier for me to drive. I made the airport in plenty of time, park at the curb and wait for them to come out of the baggage area. I notice that the gas gauge is on E and the "need fuel" light is illuminated. Great! About this time the airport cop bangs on my window and tells me I have to leave. LEAVE? I can't wait for my party? No honey, you have to drive around—no parking here, as she points to the sign. OMG, the fuel tank light indicates the tank is almost empty and I don't remember seeing a gas station in the vicinity. Apparently I have no choice, if I run out, oh well—it's meant to be. I drive as slowly as possible around and back to the curb. I still don't see them, but Shar did call and say they would be out as soon as their bag made it on the carousel. Just as the cop was asking me to drive around AGAIN, they appeared. Mike's first words were: Why did you bring THIS car? When I opened the back door, I could see why. It looked like the back of a product van—cases of stuff everywhere. They had two large suitcases plus golf clubs to fit into the space. And just wait until Mike sees the gas gauge. . . definitely should have brought his car. Somehow we managed to fit everything in the back, and find a service station before stalling. I was perched on the edge of the backseat with golf clubs behind me for the ride to Woodinville. This was a test, the one I needed to pass in order to pack VeVe for her trip north.

Chapter 70 – Drama at PetSmart

In the Seattle newspaper today a 34-year-old British guy was awarded the job that was intended for me. A six-month assignment on an island off the coast of Australia to swim, sun and relax on the beach. And, the best part? Document the experience on a blog. The pay? $111,000. There were only 35,000 applicants! I'm quite sure they were looking for me. . .

Days run together with all the activities, but dinner at Robin's was delicious. She and Joe grilled filet mignons wrapped in bacon—she really knows how to plan a menu> Maybe this is why she balked at my Red Robin's suggestion. Shrimp, edamame, snow peas, monkey bread made with Italian herbs that looked fabulous (I resisted), and Grandma's hot and cheesy potato salad (again I resisted but I know how good it is). Dessert—grilled bananas with Haagen-Dazs vanilla ice cream and chopped nuts. I love to watch people eat. It's so much better than me doing it! It was good being with my Seattle peeps. This beautiful, sunny night on the deck in West Seattle was perfect.

The next day Sharon took me to a large estate auction in the warehouse district in downtown Seattle. What fun, and so many bargains! I told her before going that I could not buy anything because there was not a smidgen of space left in VeVe. Good thing I didn't know about THESE sales when I first got here in October. Otherwise, I would need a truck to get my stuff back to Alaska! I'm at the pre-sale before the bidding starts and I see a man that looks familiar, so I follow him around in the aisle. Finally, I said: *"Max?"* and he said, " Yes." *"Remember me?"* and he responds with, *"Remind me."* Prudhoe Bay, OMG.

I worked with this man in 1980 on the pipeline. We discover neither one of us lives in Seattle, and are both just visiting. What is the likelihood of running into someone I worked with 29 years ago, in a strange city, at an estate auction in the warehouse district? A blast from a past life, and I have to wonder what that's about.

Mike's sister and spouse arrived from Maryland for a few days. I met them in 1998 at the New York City Fancy Food Show where we all worked for Sharon and Mike at their booth, and drank together at night. It was good to reconnect. They invited me to visit them on Kent Island where they have a nice Italian friend they want me to meet—good looking, sense of humor, large boat on Chesapeake Bay, and Type A. OMG, don't know about the Type A personality but a visit to Maryland is a good thought.

The only real drama in Woodinville was taking OgDog to PetSmart for a bath and grooming. He FELL off the grooming table—approximately 4 feet to the concrete floor! Can you believe it? I stressed the fact he was elderly and feeble. How could this have happened? Big lesson learned for me. I will NEVER again take him anywhere and drop him off. Next time I'll stay and watch, but it definitely won't be PetSmart. The good news is he appears to be okay. Fingers crossed.

My last stop is Gail's studio in Issaquah. I love the energy in this space. We have a cup of tea, look at her new work and I collect my birthday mask that I made back in November—something else to fit in a bulging VeVe! Tomorrow we are out of here. Goodbye Seattle and all my good friends. It's been a blast. Until next time!

Part VII

North to Alaska

Never stop wondering
Never stop wandering

Chapter 71 – Going Home

Dressed in only shorts, a long-sleeved T-shirt, sweater and flip-flops, it's a bit chilly when the wind hits me in British Columbia. Five hundred and fifty miles took eleven hours. It's hard to make good time on a two-lane road through the Canadian Rockies. Winding through small towns, the speed limit is reduced to 50 kmh, essentially 30 mph. I love the crisp air, the smoky smell mixed with pine, and the open road. No freeways on this trip. We left Woodinville this morning around 10 after running two miles, walking the dogs, feeding the dogs, and stuffing VeVe. One more thing to fit in the car would have been over the top! She is packed to the max. The dogs are in their beds sitting on top the collection of les trés jours and when they sit up, their heads touch the ceiling. They definitely have a dog's eye view of the road. They could really care less because when the car is moving, they are sleeping. My dogs became road dogs early on in our treks across the U.S. If I am driving for more than 15 minutes, they know it's a road trip and settle in for the duration, making them perfect travel-mates.

On the road again, where thoughts run rampant without distraction—I-5 to WA342, crossing the border at Abbotsford rather than Vancouver—much smaller and easier to get through. We will connect to Hwy. 1-E to 97N, which will eventually take us to Hwy. 1 in Whitehorse, and on to Alaska Highway 1, all the way to the end of the road in Homer—approximately 2,400 miles.

Entering British Columbia I feel connected to the terrain, one that I am so familiar with. Breathtaking mountains, steep, S-shaped curved roads, wildlife signs for elk, caribou and moose, and towns few and far between. HOME. I'm going home, to a place where I belong. . . as Daughtry sings. As I'm driving, this song keeps playing over and over in my head. I know this is what I need to be doing at this moment.

REWIND forty years ago, May 1969. . . war protests, Abbie Hoffman, Jimi Hendrix, Janis Joplin and the counterculture movement – sex, drugs and rock 'n roll. I missed it all. I was a teenage wife with a military husband and a 7-month-old baby boy driving to Alaska in a 1967 Ford Fairlane convertible—a convertible to Alaska? Well. . . When the two of us became three, we traded our 1962 Corvette for a more practical car, the Ford convertible.

Uncle Sam had finally given us our overseas assignment—Elmendorf Air Force Base, Anchorage, Alaska. We had fully expected Vietnam and felt grateful to be going to Alaska together. However, West Virginia to Alaska was the other side of the world where national news was delayed at least two days. Alaska was indeed remote.

The trip north was wicked; dirt and gravel, with ruts so deep that replacing tires was the norm, and finding a gas station when you needed one was a challenge. Prices were outrageous compared to the rest of the country. Instead of a four-to-five-day trip, it was at least 10 days in 1969. We kept our baby boy covered under a screen with a blanket on top so he wouldn't inhale the red dust that coated our bodies, our hair, and the entire inside of our car. What is now Liard Hot Springs, a must-see RV resort/spa on the highway, was a small pool that smelled like rotten eggs with a bench in the middle for soaking your feet after a hard day on the road driving 40 mph, at best. Things certainly have changed. Now the road is paved, with passing lanes and/or four lanes. My youngest son and his family will be moving to Wasilla, Alaska, in June, exactly 40 years later, driving this same road with their son. Ironically, history seems to be repeating itself.

I have made this trip many times but have never written about it. Maybe that's why I can't remember where I stop, and how long it actually takes from trip to trip. I realize OgDog made his first trip down the Alaska Highway at 4 months old, and since then he has made 14 trips either north or south on Route 97. He turns 16 on this trip, May 11th. Having said that, it means I have driven this road 15 times in 40 years! Alaska is home to me. I essentially grew up here, raised a family, graduated from college and have spent the better part of my adult life in this land. How could I possibly leave it for good? I will continue to travel but realize that no matter how long I stay away, when I return, I'm home.

The dogs are happy to sleep most of the day on their comfy bed made out of vintage treasures. We pass through Hell's Gate, with a restaurant on the left called Elvis Rocks Café—full of memorabilia. We then pass Jackass Mountain Summit and it feels like the top of the world. I stop for gas in Clinton and realize I am starved; nothing but an apple today and it's 3 p.m. I bought a package of Capicola ham and moutarde forte, making ham roll-ups while driving—sure cleared out the sinuses. It rained much of the day and when we reached Williams Lake the sun came out and I knew there had to be a rainbow. Sure enough, right behind me there it was—not one, but two!

We drove until half-past 9 and stopped in Prince George at

the first motel we saw, the Carmel Motor Inn. The sun was just dropping below the horizon. Ahhh, the land of the Midnight Sun. It's a good thing because VeVe is rebelling— both headlights are completely out! The only thing that works are the bright lights and the truckers keep flashing me. This car is telling me that she is indeed tired and ready to be back in Homer where life is much slower with fewer miles to cover. By the time I feed the dogs and walk to the restaurant next door, they are closing. Never mind, not that hungry anyhow. More of the ham and moutarde for dinner plus Market Spice Tea from Seattle. That will do just fine

.

Chapter 72 – A Pushy Basset Hound Called DoDog

Prince George, B.C., to Fort Nelson, B.C. – 500 miles.

Small correction from day 1: I have traveled this road 16 times instead of 15, OK? And 14 of these trips have been made since 1995! That's a lot of driving south and north. Maybe I can't make up my mind. Or maybe I just like to drive. I forgot about 1988 when I returned to Alaska from the Bay area with an insignificant other—maybe that's why I forgot the trip. The best part was my boys traveling with us driving a tan VW Beetle, making faces when they passed us, mooning us in the middle of the road when we rounded a curve in the Yukon, and going out to get pizza in Whitehorse and returning hours later—the pizza was cold, but the pool game was awesome.

I actually ran a mile this morning before leaving Prince George. I didn't want to leave the dogs unattended at the motel room for long. It was late when we checked in and I just forgot to mention I had dogs, and they didn't ask. I exchanged my shorts for sweats this morning. Beautiful blue skies and crisp weather here in B.C., but dark clouds moving in. Looks like rain farther north, great weather for driving. There are still spotty patches of snow along the road, but it's mostly gone for the season. Or at least let's hope so.

We are on Route 97 north until we reach Chetwynd, where we take a shortcut on Route 29 connecting again to the Alaska Highway just north of Fort St. John. It's raining cats and dogs—well, mostly dogs in VeVe. Most of the day Zippy manages to slither into the front seat next to OgDog, who doesn't seem to mind at all. Usually he snarls at her, but not today. She made herself especially small, curled up into a fetal position. So Luce is on my lap, Zippy and Og in the passenger seat—wait a minute. I now have three dogs in the front with me, and Woody is in the back all by himself. Soon Og moves to the back with Woody and then Zippy makes herself known. No more small basset but instead a stretched-out one, covering the entire seat, with her head on the gear shift.

I can't handle it. It's too crowded up here so I try scooting her to the back. She thinks she has rights now and refuses to go, until I stop the car and literally force her in the back. She is by far the most stubborn dog I have ever had. For the rest of the day she continues to challenge me by trying to return to the passenger seat at every opportunity, pissing me off so I end up yelling at her and the spaniels all run to their bed in the back. Like my mother used to say: *"Give her an inch and she will take a mile."* I see what she meant . . . My arm is stretched across to the passenger seat so she's not able to slither between the seats without me knowing. She is resting her head on my elbow and gently pushing down. GAWD! She can be exasperating, and adorable at the same time. Who will give up first?

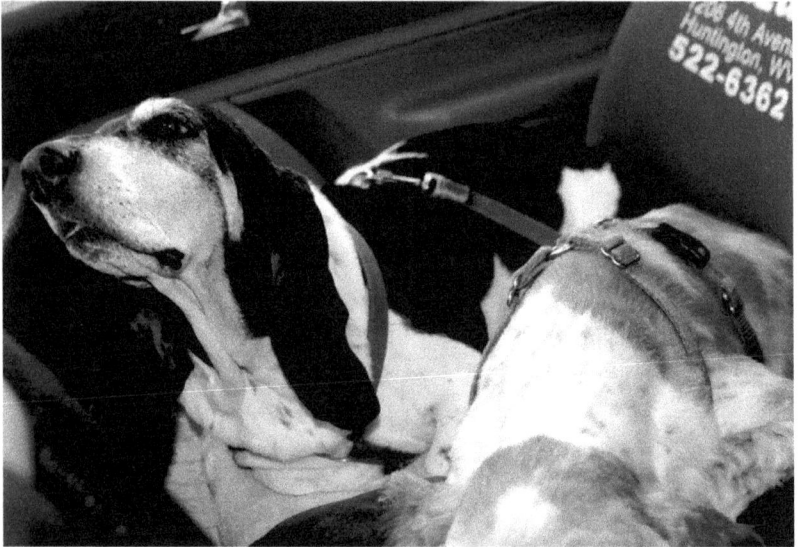

There is a liberating sense of freedom and wild abandonment in the wilderness—a connection with the vastness of the universe—few rules and not many cars or people. People smoke where they want, drive as fast as they want, pee alongside the road, and generally live and let live in this remote area. It's hard to say how much it has to do with being Canadian, or merely living outside the norm—whatever that is. Give it another month, when tourist season kicks in, and the road will be bustling with fifth-wheels, motorhomes, vans, motorcycles—you name it. Capitalists. No doubt the wildness will be replaced with a sense of conformity and political correctness. I am curious about the so-called recession and how that might impact travel north this summer.

I remember a trip south in 1995 where I was not exactly politically correct. It was a beautiful fall day in October, when I crossed the border into Canada and made a beeline to the closest place to buy beer. Canadian beer—can't remember which one but it doesn't matter. The bartender recommended it. I bought a six-pack, put it in my cooler and continued on to Whitehorse (another few hours), sipping away. OMG, drinking and driving? Yep, in the '70s it was the norm. But wait, this is the '90s!

I finished the beer while driving Free Willie (my panel van), singing at the top of my lungs with John Secada on the stereo—while the dogs slept. I stopped for dinner in Whitehorse, and probably had a couple more beers with the pizza while the dogs waited patiently in the van for their share. Afterwards, I made it a few more miles before realizing I was now too tired to drive; eating pizza always does that to me. We pull Free Willie off the road GAWD knows where, kill the engine, lock the doors, crawl into the bed in the back, and go to sleep for the night.

Around 3 a.m. a booming noise jolted me upright in bed, startling the dogs into their frantic bark mode. Rain was pouring in from the air vent above the bed—the middle of our quilt was soaked. WTF? I cautiously looked outside for any obvious critters in the black void surrounding Free Willie, and slowly eased the door open. The wind caught the door panel, jerking it back just as the vent cover flew off the roof and began bouncing across the tundra. Running out in the torrential downpour, I was able to grab the cover and get back inside in a flash. Obviously unable to put it back on the roof now, I had to come up with a plan. All the while I was thinking, thank God it was the wind and not a bear that ripped it off the roof! With duct tape and a plastic bag I was able to stop the rain for the moment and get back to the real issue at hand—getting back to sleep. The next morning the sun came out and dried the quilt. I was able to reattach the air vent cover and we continued on our way.

As I reminisce about past adventures, we are rolling on toward Fort Nelson—a likely spot to stop for the night. The problem on the highway is towns are few and far between, so if we don't stay in Fort Nelson it is at least another 250 miles to Watson Lake—too far. Besides that, I have the perfect rustic cabin in mind where we always stay. Pioneer Inn, here we come (and it is nothing like the one in Maui). We are tired and ready to crash when we pull in. But wait a minute, there is a "closed" sign on the door. This can't be. I knock on the door and see the owner; well, at least he used to be the owner. He tells me they have sold the place and are in the process of moving out. Can't I stay this one night? Sorry, but the electricity has been turned off in the cabins. Try the Shannon Motel on the way out of town. Change—one thing we can count on. Always change. So we end up at the Shannon Motel, where they charge extra for dogs. Good thing I only have one. And thank goodness they look alike, so if someone sees me walking Woody, Oggie or Luce, chances are they won't notice the difference. But the basset hound? I have to be careful with her because she always makes her presence known and looks nothing like a cocker spaniel!

I'm once again concerned about OgDog. He is panting and his stomach seems distended and tight. I give him some medicine and ask my spirit guides to help me, help him. It's not long before he is once again sleeping peacefully but not before

I call the front desk—it must be past midnight now—and ask for the local vet's phone number, just in case I need it.

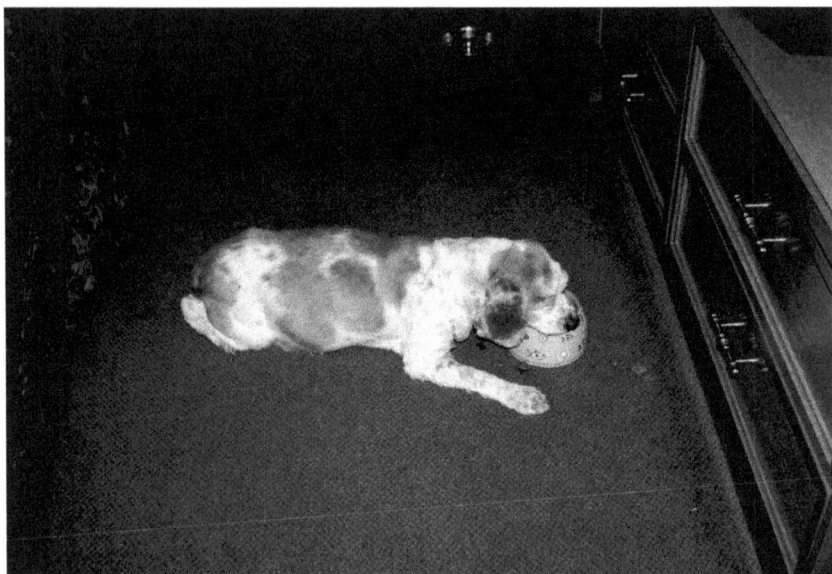

Chapter 73 – Smuggling Dogs in the Yukon

Fort Nelson, B.C. to Whitehorse, Y.T. – 550 miles.

Oggie seems better this morning; still has a distended stomach but it doesn't feel as hot. I did some research online and narrowed it down to: 1) overweight; 2) Cushing's disease; or 3) congestive heart problem, where liquid fills the abdomen, making breathing difficult. It's definitely time for a visit with our Homer Vet Clinic when we get home.

We pack the car, stop for gas and coffee and finally get on the road around 10. The sun is out and the skies are clear. No run this morning, too worried about Oggie and didn't want to leave them alone in the room. Remember, there is only one of them. I asked the front desk for a can opener for the dog food, and was on my way to pick it up after walking Luce when I see the owner's wife at my door, about to knock—flashback from Hermosillo! Yikes! Excuse me, as I run up to her and she hands me an opener that looks like it's from the '50s, at least. Surprisingly, the dogs are not barking from the other side of the door. She helps me with the can on the sidewalk but the opener does not even come close to working. She runs inside and comes back with another—not any better. Back inside for a third, and then a fourth one that finally does the job.

Imagine the time involved in the simplest things—does she ever have a need to open a can in the wilderness, I wonder. She was very helpful and I was grateful for finally getting the dog food open, and not getting busted for the one dog that is really three look-alikes, and a basset hound that demands to be noticed.

It's a quiet trip to Watson Lake where we officially enter the Yukon Territory. The dogs are settled in and Zippy is not pushing to get up front, and that is a good thing. I think about what an adventure it must have been building the original Alcan Highway back in the '40s. Men and women on a huge construction job—probably much like the Trans-Alaska Pipeline in the '70s. I was on that project and know about the hard work and camaraderie involved in a remote project of this magnitude. I could definitely write chronicles about that adventure.

In Watson Lake we stop at Café Belvedere, another regular place on the road. I order the chicken Caesar salad; hold the croutons and not too much Parmesan, thank you very much. A disappointment because, well, it's not as good as I remembered it to be—an indication of yet another change. What is the adage—the nature of existence is a ceaseless transformation.

I eat my salad on the road. I really hate doing that but I want to get to Whitehorse or beyond today, so there is no time for a sit-down lunch. The third day is always the hardest; we are tired and just want to be there. And we will actually hit the halfway point today!

A few hours later we arrive in Whitehorse and I am stiff and tired of driving—now I'm whining. Staying here is always expensive but the other option is to drive on to Haines Junction, another couple hours. I just don't have it in me, so I stop at the Airport Chalet. Been here before, and they have a motel section out back that is perfect for the dogs. That is until she tells me the price—$119 plus $10/dog, plus taxes, etc. Yikes! I stayed here last year and it was around $69. Nope, not for that section, she said, but she can put me inside the hotel, about eight doors down from the front desk, for $99, but she will wave the pet fee of $10, so it's actually $89. Did I tell her I had four dogs? Not a chance. The tricky part will be getting them past her into the room. Once we're in, we're okay for the night. Traveling with four dogs is not always easy for a Silly Woman, but somehow we always seem to manage.

I give her my credit card and park VeVe behind the hotel.

The plan is to bring my luggage and the dogs in the back door, to avoid passing the front desk. Four trips later all my stuff is in and, one by one, the dogs have arrived. We are safe for the night. The nice thing about being in a hotel is the bar and restaurant. A drink would be nice, so I head to the hotel pub to get a Scotch for the room. Not possible because of their license; you cannot bring it to your room. After much debate between the management, the bartender was finally able to make an exception and follow me to the room with my drink. I didn't want to leave the dogs alone or I could have just stayed at the pub. I feed the dogs, drink my drink and realize I need to get some food. Back to the pub, where a hockey game is in full swing on the big screen. Women fans are in the bar yelling obscenities and cheering wildly for their team, the Canucks.

I love this about Canada; they are so into their hockey. I totally get into it and order another drink while I wait for my food. Chicago Blackhawks and Vancouver Canucks—the Canucks are up! So much fun. . .brought me back to my hockey-mom days! I get my order, finish my drink and take the food back to my room. I have no idea who actually won the game. But I do know it's the Stanley Cup playoffs and there is hockey energy all over Canada!

The dogs are sacked out—not sure why they are so tired. After all, they DID sleep all day in the car. But it was cramped for them and here we have two beds, so they can stretch out. When I get on the bed they rearrange themselves to get as close to me as they can. Oggie is on my left side, Luce on my right, while Zippy and Woody work their way under the covers to the bottom of the bed, lying on my feet. Time for some much needed rest and relaxation. And tomorrow? We will cross the border into Alaska! Life is good for a Silly Woman with four dogs—posing as one— in a hotel somewhere near Whitehorse, Y.T.

Chapter 74 – The Marathon Day

Whitehorse, Y.T., to Lake Louise Lodge, Glennallen, AK. – 650 miles (OMG)

We have our second wind today and are ready for the final leg into Alaska. I pack our things and load the car, taking the dogs out of the hotel one at a time. The sun is shining but the air is still chilly. It's only 444 km to Beaver Creek (275 miles), and another 15 miles to the U.S. border.

On the drive I decide we are pretty tired of the hotel scene so once we get into Alaska we are going to find a rustic cabin in the woods to spend tonight. Lake Louise would be perfect; it's close to Glennallen and off the beaten path. The lake is huge—approximately 26 square miles of water that is frozen solid in the winter. We used to go in the spring to cross-country ski, stay in a cabin and hang out at the lodge by the fireplace. There are actually four lodges and skiing around to the other three was always great exercise and fun. Yes, Lake Louise is a good thought, but getting there is much farther than I will drive today.

Beaver Creek is a small community with some crabby people—seems like the last few times I have stopped at the grocery/gas station, people have been less than helpful; in fact, downright rude—a real contrast to the other towns along the way. This is the place to use up any Canadian money left in the wallet. I count out $6 in change so I stop and pump $6 worth of gas. When I went inside to pay, the attendant made some snide comment about the amount. I thought it was a logical way to use up the money. Where is that hockey energy, anyhow?

Can you believe it is spitting snow? Maybe that has something to do with the attitude. I get the camera out to take a picture and just that quickly the snow is gone and the sun comes out again. The road is awful—by far the worst area of the trip, lots of frost heaves that will take the bottom of a car out if going too fast. In Mexico they have speed bumps called topas. Frost heaves are similar, only bigger. Because of the road condition it takes longer than expected to go 15 miles. We finally reach the border; flash the passport to the attendant, who asks me the purpose of my trip. I smile and say: *"To get out of here for the winter."* Duh. He smiles back and says, *"Good for you,"* and waves us through—*"and welcome home,"* he adds.

Driving on to the first Alaska town, Tok. Yep, that's the name of it. When I arrive my cell phone comes to life and I have Happy Mother's Day greetings from the boys. That's right, it IS my day to celebrate! Where is that cabin in the woods? There are some cabins in Tok but they only have one that is pet friendly and it is taken for the night. Obviously someone else has the same idea. Movin' on down the road to our usual motel—their price is $89 for the night. Do we really want to stay here, or should we keep looking for a cabin? It's still early, so we move on. Glennallen is another 140 miles down the highway and I don't have a clue what they have in the way of accommodations—it's pretty small. Along the way there are a couple places offering cabins for rent, if only they were open—the season really starts on Memorial Day, so the smaller places are still closed.

A couple more hours of driving and we are in Glennallen and there is one hotel called The Caribou. It looks really fancy by

Alaska standards but I stop anyhow and go to the front desk. The conversation went something like this:

"This doesn't look like a place where I can bring my dog."

"Oh yes, you can have a dog here, for $119/night plus $10/for the dog, taxes, etc. That's the off-season price."

"Yikes! That's way more than I want to spend! That's the best you can do?"

"Well," he said, *"we do have a pipeline camp."*

"What does that mean?" He points to the ATCO trailers across the parking lot.

"I don't usually even mention it because most people won't consider staying there."

"Oh, but I have stayed in pipeline camps on the North Slope for years. I know what they are like: twin beds, sparsely furnished with a bathroom down the hall, right?" "Yep, that's it," he said, and hands me a key so I can have a look.

OMG! Déjà vu! In fact, I may have stayed in this very camp at some point in my career and I don't really want to do it again. And besides that, it's $79 for this experience!

"Well, what do you think?" he asks when I bring the key back to the desk.

"I think it's fine and I would definitely consider it for $40 but

no way will I pay $79 to stay in a place that I might have already lived in, for free. Thanks anyhow!" Movin' on.

At this point I am starting to fade and the dogs are definitely ready to be out of the car. Okay, worst-case scenario—I do know a fleabag motel (no pun intended) in Palmer that will allow the dogs—but that's another 2.5 hours down the road. At this rate it's going to be midnight before we get out of VeVe. I can't believe I'm home and can't find a place to stay for the night. I want it to be special; after all, it IS Mother's Day and I just drove over 2,000 miles! Is a cabin in the woods too much to ask, I wonder?

Back to the road. A few more miles and I see the Lake Louise cut-off to the right: Wow! Wasn't I just thinking about this place earlier today, never dreaming I would drive this far? The sign said 20 miles, so I pass on by. Immediately the adventure self screams: WHAT are you doing? Well, I'm thinking if I make the turn and drive 20 miles and they are not open, then I will have to drive 20 miles back to the main road, adding another 40 miles on to the trip to Palmer, which is already 140 miles from here.

My intuition kicks in. . . just do it, take the risk! What the hell—you want a cabin, you know they have cabins there, so go for it. What's 40 more miles at this point anyhow? True. I make a U-turn in the middle of the road! All the while thinking, if you want it bad enough, the universe will provide!

Even the dogs perk up. We drive the 20 miles, find the lodge open and we are the only guests for the night—we are ecstatic, and a bit rummy from being on the road for more hours than I care to think about. Hidden among the pine trees is the perfect rustic cabin just waiting for us. The bathroom is in the main lodge along with the bar and restaurant. The dogs are free to jump out of the car and hang with the local canines. After all, we're in the woods and Zippy can be off-leash to run free! We unpack and get settled into our Alaskan cabin. I turn the heat on, feed the dogs and then go to the lodge to feed myself a grilled chicken Caesar salad and a

Cognac at the bar. This is the perfect place for our first night back in Alaska. It feels great to be home again. Well, almost. Happy Mother's Day to me!

BTW, did I mention that out of the 16 trips I have made on the Alaska Highway, 14 were done alone with the dogs?

Woof! Woof!

Chapter 75 – Stoli the Cat, and Four Barking Dogs!

Lake Louise Lodge, Glennallen, Alaska to Anchorage, Alaska. 200-plus miles.

We wake up to a gorgeous, sunny morning. After checking at the bar to be sure no bears had been spotted in the area, we were off on a much-needed hike. All dogs off-leash! We walked over a mile, with Woody wandering off the trail and the next thing I know he is nowhere to be seen. Hopefully he will find his way back.

We take our time getting back to the lodge, finished packing the car, checked out at the front desk and were just about ready to start up VeVe when we see Woody running down the trail toward us. That's good. I thought I would have to drive up the road so he could hear the car before he would come out of the woods. We get started toward Anchorage around noon. I've decided to spend the night and visit some friends before going on to Homer tomorrow.

I make a few phone calls, do some planning and end up at Mike's house just at the time he gets home from work. We have not seen Mike since he visited Casa Miramar. He is so gracious, inviting me (and all my dogs) into his home for the night, although Stoli the cat is not too pleased with this decision at all. Especially when the dogs want to chase him through the house. Mike fixed us gin and tonics and we sat on the deck in the sun enjoying the weather. The sun was so warm that I almost (almost) put on my bathing suit, but I knew as it got later I would definitely be cold. It's nice, but it's NOT Mexico weather!

Stoli is on Mike's lap enjoying the sun when Zippy jumps up to say hi. The cat freaks, Zippy starts barking, getting the other dogs in the action, and total chaos follows. Mike held Stoli (big mistake) as he clawed his way free, jumping off and flying across the lawn with the dogs in hot pursuit! Lots of nasty scratch marks on Mike's arms, as I go find the peroxide. Once everything calms down, it's time for the dogs to go to their room and Stoli— still hissing his discontentment at having the dogs in his space—to resume his position as top cat of the household. Sorry Mike, dogs will be dogs and cats will be cats.

Mike has a neighbor that's an artist and he wanted me to meet her, so after a couple drinks we knock on her door. Who needs an invite anyhow, this is Alaska. He was right, Lucky and I hit it off right away and know lots of the same people in Anchorage. She makes papier-mâché dogs that are whimsical and fun. But when she showed me her costume room, I was hooked. So many clothes, hats, wigs, boots, shoes. She said this is the room she comes to when she's going out for the evening to decide who she wants to be. Maybe I need a bigger house with a dress-up room.

Later, Mike fixed a halibut dinner with fiddlehead ferns, and opened a bottle of red wine. Keep in mind I haven't had wine since January. What a treat—it was a delicious Russian River Cabernet. That's what abstaining does—makes it even better than what I remember. As the Brits say, I was in my cups for the evening—lost my nose ring and I'll be damned if I could find it. Probably because I couldn't focus. . .

The next morning after coffee we were on the road again, destined for our home in Homer later today. Goodbye Stoli—you are no doubt delighted to see the backsides of four gregarious dogs walking out your front door.

Chapter 76 - Home Again, Home Again, Jiggity Jog!

Anchorage, Alaska to the End of the Road, Homer, Alaska. 220 miles.

Today we will really be home in Homer. But first I have friends to see in Anchorage. Met up with a special person for coffee at his hotel, stopped at my friend Judy's office to say hi and invite her to Homer for a weekend this summer, and then met my buddy Chuck for lunch. When we were deciding where to go, he asked me if I liked Mexican food—can you imagine? Even he said that was a dumb question! Duh. I've only been in Mexico for four months! He is headed out of Alaska for Oregon tomorrow and wanted to pick my brain about road conditions, routes, gas prices, etc. Funny, but we almost passed on the road—so glad he's starting a trip and not me. We will be happy to get off the road for a while.

After lunch the dogs are ready to get on with it. We get in

VeVe and head for Homer. The sun is shining over Cook Inlet on this beautiful spring day. The drive from Anchorage to Homer is known to be one of the most spectacular scenic drives in the U.S. I only have one stop to make at Sweet Magnolia's in Soldotna—a head shop. I know they would have nose rings and if I don't get one fast, the piercing hole will close. Sure enough, I bought three and asked for a mirror. It is difficult to get the post in my nose because they are so small, and the lighting in the store is dim. I asked the young man at the counter if he could help me. He tried, but it wouldn't go through and now it is burning and my eyes are watering. I will just keep trying. By this time I'm bleeding a bit. I get in the car, look in the rearview mirror where I can see much better, hold my breath and just push it on through. In a few more hours it would have needed re-piercing and I left the piercing surgeon behind in Guaymas. No worries, it's done now.

An hour later we are dropping over Baycrest Hill into the town of Homer. The view is breathtaking—blue water framed with snowcapped mountains. The dogs start getting antsy when we start up East Hill Road. By the time we turn onto Katie Jean Circle, Zippy is hanging out the window, panting. They know where we are.

We were welcomed home by five visiting doggies barking at the door. Sophie is a regular; she's been coming to Tails-By-The-Bay Dog Camp since she was eight weeks old. But the confusion is a little much for her; she's not sure what's going on and who we are. She's a bit standoffish but after a few sniffs seems to finally recognize us. The house is spotless but the cupboards are bare. The dogs get settled in, the dogsitters and I settle up and when they leave, I make a trip to the grocery store. OMG, talk about sticker-price shock! I need to get an extra job just to pay for food here. I knew it would be shocking but I was not prepared for this much difference—milk $3.50/gallon (on sale from $3.99), eggs $3.29/dozen, fresh salad greens $8/pound, OJ $5.99/half gallon. Aye yi yi! I will continue to lose weight at this rate.

I spend the evening getting readjusted to my house and possessions, and just enjoy being home. We decide on sleeping in the downstairs bedroom because it's in the back of the house and is cool from the breeze that flows through the screen. When I look at the clock I can't believe it's 2 a.m. already. It must be the caffeine from the Market Spice Tea! I have to go to sleep because I have Jessie, the husky, arriving at 7:30 a.m. for day care.

I am up at 6 sharp walking the dogs and going for a run. It's like I'm in training all over again because there is nowhere to run near the house that isn't uphill. If I just pace myself, I will do fine—something Antonio taught me. Jessie arrives at 7:30 and is added to the pack of Paxton the retriever, Zip the corgi, Ruby the Labrador retriever, and Sophie the golden— along with the resident dogs, OgDog, Woody, Lucy and Zippy. Business continues as normal. I haven't even been here 24 hours but already it feels like I never left.

There is truly no place like home, especially for a Silly Woman, four traveling canines and a white VW Beetle called VeVe. Content to be back safe and sound in their own bed at the moment, until the wanderlust hits again, and takes them off on yet another adventure. Stay tuned. . .

Part VIII

Diet of A Silly Woman

Disclaimer: This information should not be used for diagnosing or treating a health problem. Not all diet and exercise plans suit everyone. You should always consult your licensed healthcare provider before starting a diet, taking any form of prescription medication, or embarking on any fitness or weight training program. The creators and content providers disclaim any liability or loss in connection with the information provided here.

This diet plan was easy for me to follow and I never felt better and more fit in my life. I lost a total of 17 pounds over an 11-week period and was told during my last weigh-in with the nutritionist that I was at my ideal weight and did not need to lose anymore—beautiful music to my ears and the perfect ending of a fabulous winter in Mexico.

I found the diet to be simple, straightforward and easy to maintain. The challenge was to find various ways to prepare the meats. For example, I crumbled hamburger meat and used taco seasonings to create a taco salad, minus the cheese, guacamole and sour cream. I prepared ground beef with balsamic vinegar that I rolled up in lettuce leaves. Seasonings and fresh herbs kept the diet plan interesting! I also had mucho chicken fajitas without the tortillas. Fajitas are served plain in Mexico, without all the extras such as cheese, guacamole and sour cream.

In my opinion, the key for this diet to be successful is determination and perseverance—without cheating like Maggie consistently did. Truth was she really didn't need to lose any weight so she wasn't that serious about it. This is probably the type of diet that if you do cheat, you might gain weight. It's the combination that seems to work.

There are few rules and no measuring portions, ounces, etc., or counting calories or carbohydrates. The following information applies to every weekly plan.

Exercise helps to prevent cardiovascular illness and eliminates stress.

Staying hydrated (drinking water) helps to improve metabolism, reduce fat and improve digestion.

In case of constipation or poor digestion, try adding fiber to your diet.

If irritation or headache occurs, try an orange juice or fruit that day, and avoid fat.

Chew all food slowly and thoroughly.

The feeling of thirst is the guide that we must consume more water.

Drink water with lemon or natural water.

Coffee and tea are okay to drink with any meal.

CAN USE:
Sugar substitutes
Trident gum
Sugar-free refreshments (4 per week)
Substitutes for coffee: Coffee-mate, Lemac, Lautrec in place of cream or milk
Light salad dressings such as Ranch, 1000 Island, or

oil/vinegar
Beverages such as vodka, tequila, gin, rum, whiskey
Safflower oil, vegetable oil or Pam

TO AVOID:
Corn, beets, avocado, grapes
Beer and wine
Corn oil
Beans and rice
Potatoes

Bon Appétit!

Silly Woman Diet Plan, Week 1
Eat only what is listed on the menu

Breakfast Options (2):
2 slices of light bread with light jam
1 glass of fresh-squeezed orange juice
OR
1 bowl of cereal with light milk (Cornflakes, Special K, All Bran)
1 glass fresh-squeezed orange juice

Between Meals:
Jicama and cucumber with lemon or salsa

Lunch:
Steak or chicken
Green salad

Dinner:
Any kind of meat with salad

Silly Woman Diet Plan, Week 2
Eat only what is listed on the menu

Breakfast:
1 large glass of fresh-squeezed OJ or grapefruit juice
2 eggs with ham

Between Meals:
1 fruit (avoid mango, banana and grapes)
Cucumber with lemon

Lunch:
Vegetable soup
Beef, chicken or fish, the amount you want
Light Jell-O
Green salad

Dinner:
Green salad with or without meat (chicken, ham, tuna)

Silly Woman Diet Plan, Week 3
Eat only what is listed on the menu

Breakfast Options (2):

Light yogurt and fruit of the season, the amount you want
OR
Cereal (Special K, All Bran or Corn Flakes) with light milk

Between Meals:

Jicama and cucumber or fruit (avoid mango, banana and grapes)

Lunch:

Vegetable soup
Chicken or fish (not breaded)
Light Jell-O

Dinner:

Salad with chicken breast or tuna

Silly Woman Diet Plan, Week 4
Eat only what is listed on the menu

Breakfast:
2 eggs with ham
Fruit juice of the season

Between Meals:
Orange or papaya

Lunch:
Roast beef or chicken and salad

Dinner Options (2):
3 slices melon or papaya with liquids
OR
1 slice of toast with cottage cheese

Silly Woman Diet Plan, Week 5
Eat only what is listed on the menu

Breakfast:
Bowl of cereal – All Bran, Corn Flakes, or Special K with light milk
Fresh-squeezed orange or grapefruit juice

Between Meals Options (2):
1 fruit
OR
Light yogurt

Lunch:
Meat of any kind
Vegetables (in soup or salad)
Light Jell-O

Between Meals:
Apple

Dinner:
Meat of any kind with green salad

Silly Woman Diet Plan, Week 6
Eat only what is listed on the menu

Breakfast Option:
Smoothie—blend one-half papaya or melon, light milk and ice
Add cinnamon and vanilla to taste

Between Meals:
1 fruit juice in season (avoid mango, banana and grape)

Lunch:
Lean chicken breast or roast beef
Green salad with steamed vegetables
Fresh-squeezed grapefruit juice

Dinner:
Smoothie—blend one-half papaya or melon, light milk and ice
Add cinnamon and vanilla to taste

Silly Woman Diet Plan, Week 7
Eat only what is listed on the menu

Breakfast Options (2):
One hot cake with honey or jam
OR
Bowl of cereal (Special K, All Bran, Corn Flakes) with light milk

Between Meals:
Apple or pear

Lunch:
Vegetable soup
Beef, chicken or fish

Dinner:
Salad with beef or chicken

Silly Woman Diet Plan, Week 8
Eat only what is listed on the menu

Breakfast Options (2):
2 eggs and 1 slice whole wheat bread or one corn tortilla
OR
Tuna or chicken sandwich
1 cup of light milk
Seasonal fruit

Between Meals:
Jicama and cucumber with salsa

Lunch:
Chicken, beef or fish in soup or stew
Green salad with lettuce, radish and cucumber

Dinner:
Green salad with chicken breast or tuna

Silly Woman Diet Plan, Week 9
Eat only what is listed on the menu

Breakfast Options (3):
Yogurt and fruit
OR
Eggs and fresh-squeezed orange juice
OR
Cereal with light milk

Between Meals:
Apple, pear or jicama

Lunch:
Chicken or fish
Vegetables

Dinner:
Green salad with fish, meat or cold turkey

Silly Woman Diet Plan, Week 10
Eat only what is listed on the menu

Breakfast:
2 slices toast w/marmalade

Between Meals:
Jicama, apple or pear

Lunch:
Chicken or seafood soup with vegetables

Dinner:
Tuna salad, chicken, seafood, meat or cold turkey
Green salad

Silly Woman Diet Plan, Week 11
Eat only what is listed on the menu

Breakfast Options (2):
2 eggs
1 slice whole wheat bread or a corn tortilla
OR
Eggs and fresh-squeezed orange juice
1 seasonal fruit

Between Meals:
1 fruit (avoid mango, banana and grapes)

Lunch:
Steak or chicken
Green salad

Dinner:
Green salad with chicken or tuna

www.ingramcontent.com/pod-product-compliance
Lightning Source LLC
Chambersburg PA
CBHW061817040426
42447CB00012B/2693